# CHAPTER 30

*Life Lessons from
a Perfectly Imperfect Woman*

**by Nofisa Caseman**

Chapter 30: Life Lessons from a Perfectly Imperfect Woman

Self-Development

First Printed in United Kingdom 2019

Published by Conscious Dreams Publishing
www.consciousdreamspublishing.com

Author/Cover Photos by Andrea Tajti

Cover Design by Andrii Lenchuk

Photo of Jevon Paraisy (page 205) by Jemella Binns
www.mellzphotography.co.uk

ISBN: 978-1-912551-64-4

Dear reader, I believe in you
When everything around feels dark and that nobody understands
what you are going through, remember, the sun will always rise
Learn to trust a better day will always come your way and continue
to pursue your goals and dreams. They were given to you
for a reason

*'Every man has power to lift the fog in his life. It may be a fog of
lack of money, love, happiness, or health. Give thanks for the sun'*

**~ Florence Scovel Shinn ~**

# Helping One Woman at a Time

I had a coaching session with Nofisa and was struck by her lovely and compassionate attitude. She helped me to see clearly what it is that is blocking me today to move forward. And awareness is the first step to improve my life. I highly recommend her to anyone who wants to stop using excuses and look into their truth to improve their life and business.

**Sabrina Fusaro**

I had the pleasure of working with Nofisa over a number of weeks. I needed clarity and felt stuck after coming through a dark place and losing my confidence, self-esteem and, unfortunately, who I was. I was struggling to find me again and Nofisa helped me go back to who I was, a happy place, to love me, flaws and all, in order to keep moving forward. She helped me realise I was somebody special and able to do anything I wanted. I believe that now, because initially I struggled with that, but she helped me see things differently, visualise and journal, which I love! I am taking the steps to be me again and can definitely feel a change. Thank you Nofisa.

**Diana Richards**

My time with Nofisa has been transformational. She is masterful at bringing forth the power buried within. She helped me release suppressed anger, forgive those who had made me self-doubt and self-sabotage, gave me resources and asked what I was committed to doing to feel the power I know I have inside. She also held me accountable [for sticking to my goals]. Nofisa is a life-changing coach that really pulls the superpower out of women.

**Lynn Hudorovich**

One session with Nofisa left me empowered and confident. I had clarity on why I had not achieved a particular goal.

**Donna Henry**

The past six weeks of coaching with Nofisa has helped me become the woman I was meant to be! She has helped me figure out what has been holding me back.

**Megan Aguilar**

I had a life-changing experience today speaking with Nofisa Caseman. I didn't even realise how much I was holding myself back. Talk about a lightbulb moment! Amazing.

**Tasha Campbell**

# Dedication

First and foremost, thank you to each person who has supported me in some way, shape or form on this perfectly imperfect journey called life. I appreciate you!

This book is dedicated to Jevon; because of you, I have learned so much about myself, my strengths, my weaknesses and who I am as a woman. Becoming a mother was the wake-up call I needed to begin to build a new foundation, one where I am a perfectly imperfect woman living with purpose.

Motherhood has been the most interesting, challenging, powerful, funny, stressful and magical six years of my life. With you I have learned the true meaning of unconditional love.

Thank you for choosing me as your guardian.

# Contents

## PART FOUR

## PART FIVE

# Introduction

The idea for this book came only recently, as I began to realise age thirty was just around the corner and I felt far from ready to enter a new decade. Thoughts around not being where I hoped I would be by the time I reached this age made me worry and doubt what I was capable of. I constantly compared myself with others, especially those younger women on Instagram living with purpose, which I felt I was doing half-heartedly.

Then there were those feelings of meeting guy after guy after guy after guy (and breathe), yet never really connecting to any of them on a deeper level, which left me questioning if I was 'asking for too much' and if someone I desired would be in my life soon.

Adding to my frustration as I approached thirty was not having my own place, after moving two years earlier to live in London with my mother. However, it did not stop there. I had also begun to feel like I was no longer sharing my light with individuals fighting to see clearly in their darkest hour. In short, regardless of what my Instagram feed displayed – when I dragged myself out of my self-imposed shackles long enough to post an uplifting picture or video – I was fighting an inner battle, and most days my negative ego was winning this war.

Having listened to many females share their individual stories and challenges of life, I know I am not the only one who has experienced this war within. You've been there too, right? Those days when you are so focused on change and moving forward towards your goals yet, somehow, fear consumes your mind, body and soul to the point of paralysis and you stop. You stop doing what works, you stop allowing the good feelings to circulate your entire being and then, slowly but surely, you begin to retreat. Self-doubt clouds your once-focused mind, your insecurities scream: 'I don't feel deserving of this good life' and, eventually, procrastination replaces action. Stuck is how you feel and trapped is what you believe you are. I admit, I had allowed the circumstances of my life to play me, beat me down and disrupt my positive mental attitude.

**Until one day, I began to realise I was so stuck on me!**

I was constantly focused on what was not going right in my life and as a result creating a mountain of drama and despair out of temporary appearances. That's right, I was super-stressing over circumstances I could control and a reality I had the power to change. On the one hand I felt stuck, yet on the other, I was aware I had everything needed to move forward. I just had to decide, followed by major action in addition to telling my fears and doubts to fuck right off.

## Why Chapter 30?

After reading Kevin Hart's authentic, hilarious and thought-provoking book *I Can't Make This Up*, I instinctively knew it was my time to share the good, the powerful, the painful and uncomfortable lessons of life that have brought me to where I am today. So, it is with great pleasure that I introduce *Chapter 30*; thirty life lessons from your girl right here to mark my thirtieth year on this planet. My hope for you reading this is to become aware of how much control we have over our lives. I want to be so honest with you throughout this book, showing where I have made mistakes, got in my own way, allowed fear to keep me from taking action and self-sabotaged big time. But I also want to show where I have overcome major obstacles, healed my wounds, forgiven, embraced opportunity and achieved the goals I set myself. I hope the lessons I learned will create conversations that spark change, prompt healing and the development of self-confidence for so many.

Remember these are the life lessons I want to share with you. They are the things I have learned, healed, cried about, witnessed, experienced and overcome. I am still navigating my way through this amazing process called life, so here is my final word and disclaimer before we begin.

## 1. I Am Not Your Guru

I write, I speak, I coach, I teach and see myself as a contributor to the world of intentional improvement, through sharing my own learnings. When I first began teaching, I felt like I had to know so much more before I could share my voice and story. An awesome gentleman named Wade soon showed me how wrong I was and that, in fact, I was ready to begin contributing to a cause so close to my heart. I am no different to you. I am a girl from South London, following her bliss and heart's desires, helping others do the same. Alongside my book, I invite anyone to get the support or professional help they need to move forward. This is not a substitute.

## 2. I Am Still on a Journey

We all are! Until the day our mortal experience ends, we will learn, develop and grow (if you are not growing, slowly your soul is dying). I can safely say I do not have all the answers, and I am learning to trust more each day that all will be OK in life. There is power in surrender.

## 3. I Am a Perfectly Imperfect Woman

I love that I make mistakes, am awkward in my own way, talk to myself, enjoy my own company (as well as being in the presence of others) and am still trying to figure out motherhood. I absolutely love sharing my journey in the hopes that it will inspire someone, somewhere to show up for their life's work in a perfectly imperfect way. So, take what you can from this book and leave what may not apply to you. I only ask that you have an open mind as you dive into these pages. Having forced myself to grow in a short space of time, through daring to go to the places of unhealed wounds, limiting beliefs and resentments which I could not shake, I invite you to sit back, grab a journal, a glass of wine and dive right in.

**Love, Nofisa**

## A Final Note Before We Begin

At the end of each chapter, I have included several exercises for you to dive into the subject a little deeper. It is your choice as to how you approach this. Feel free to read through the whole book and take your time to do each *'Let Us Explore'* section after, or take the time to do the exercises once you complete each chapter.

*\*Some names have been changed to protect the privacy of certain individuals\**

# PART ONE

# Life Lessons
# on Building a Stronger Foundation

I had just turned eighteen when I began to take my life seriously and think about what I wanted my future to look like. Throughout high school, I was labelled the aggressive girl with attitude and, aged thirteen, my mum was so tired of my drama, she seriously considered sending me to Jamaica to live with my aunt, hoping I would straighten up and return a changed woman. No way was I getting shipped out of London, so I pleaded to remain with her, promising to be better.

However, by the time I was seventeen I had been excluded from high school three times, dropped out of two colleges within four months and sent a boy to the hospital to have stitches in his head by throwing a metal umbrella at him, after he threw a snowball in my face. Although it stung like hell, I overreacted and as I saw blood pour from Michael's head, I instantly felt remorse, apologised and took him for medical support. It was very awkward to tell the receptionist that although I brought him to get cleaned up, I created the head injury, and as soon as the confession was out, I was sent to the Principal's office knowing fully what was about to happen.

I like to think I was generally a sweet young woman, however my temper at times was out of control to the point I requested anger-management support at the age of fifteen. I knew what I was doing and how I was behaving wasn't working for me, yet I had no idea how to change my thoughts, attitude, feelings and behaviour. To others it felt like I was a problem with no solution.

The driving force behind this change I made at eighteen was a break-up. After two years of an intense relationship, I ended what I had with Daniel because I was so over the constant arguing and my gut told me if I stayed much longer, we would likely become violent towards each other. I was not down for that experience so, as much as it hurt to say goodbye, I did. What screwed me up, (yet was the catalyst for starting to take my life seriously), was that it didn't take Daniel long to sleep with someone I knew. It was a girl we went to school with. A friend broke the news one night with intimate details of their connection. My chest began to tighten, my eyes swelled with salty tears and rage pierced my soul as I rushed her off the phone and began to dial Daniel's number. As soon as he picked up, I went in: 'Is it true?' 'How could you do this?' 'Why her?' As if it made any difference who he slept with.

Silence.

Then came his answer, which felt like a slap in the face followed by the most painful after-burn I could not escape from. 'What does it matter to you?' he blurted. 'We aren't together anymore.' He was right. I had no say! Daniel was not my guy. I felt like somebody had ripped my heart from my chest and I had to go on living with a darkness where it once beat. I vowed revenge, but this was not the type of revenge you may be thinking.

I was a peculiar young woman, and from that day forward I made a promise to be the best version of myself because, in my eyes, that would be the sweetest revenge. I remember proudly sharing my plan of attack with my mother, but she didn't pay my words much attention, so I got on with my plan, quietly working on myself.

I began reading, taking myself to networking events, studying success principles and applying the law of attraction to my life without really knowing what I was doing. I was simply determined to create a life I loved. I started to focus on winning in life and it was paying off nicely. In the four years after the break-up, I graduated college with a triple distinction in Travel & Tourism and went on to study Marketing at Birmingham, where I graduated with a first-class degree. I then got offered an internship with Virgin Atlantic in Newark, New Jersey, and began learning pole dance, something I had wanted to do since the age of sixteen. One could say my attempts at turning my behaviour and mindset around were working rather well.

In the last twelve years especially, I have learned so much through my relationships, pursuing different jobs, starting a business, motherhood, and from simply being a woman. I have begun to dive deep into metaphysics and understanding how the mind works to live my best life, confidently and unapologetically, while helping others do the same. In the first section, my goal is to share the powerful lessons that continue to support me to improve the quality of my life. Let's get straight to it.

# CHAPTER 1

# Life Lesson One

## LIVES FALL APART WHEN THEY NEED REBUILDING

*'Sometimes it takes certain things falling apart for better things to fall into place. Sometimes it takes losing what you are settling for to remind you of what you truly deserve'*

**~ Trent Shelton ~**

Life is a game which, while growing up, I didn't know how to play. Nobody told me I had the power to create a life I desired. I'm not upset, because I understand my mother couldn't have shared that information with me as she too was unaware of this truth. I believe mother was so focused on trying to survive as a single parent with two kids and a dark cloud of debt. She simply didn't know how to see past her reality, a result of her own thinking and beliefs, to learn the spiritual laws of life and the science of getting rich. They would have set her free from her struggle.

I cannot say my mother did not have access to the information that could have changed her life for the better, as we all do. Now more than ever, the principles of universal law are easily accessible for those who dare to break free from their mental chains and unleash the power of their subconscious mind to create a life they once could have only dreamed of. However, breaking free is probably the most difficult aspect of the journey as you, like me, will be asked to:

- *Challenge your belief system*
- *Let go of stories and ideas you have held your whole life*
- *Speak your truth*
- *Look to current appearances as false*
- *Dig deep into your past to uncover the unhealed wounds that keep you stuck in repetitive patterns that no longer serve you*
- *Question almost everything you've been taught*

That, my friend, is no walk in the park, yet who we become on the other side is always worth it.

***

At the age of eighteen, it was clear redirection was necessary for my growth. The break-up with Daniel, which felt so hard to go through, provided a space for me to reflect, dream, plan and work hard towards my desires. However, that would not be the last time my life would feel like it was falling apart. But this was necessary to push me to my next level.

I am a mother to a beautiful six-year-old boy and believe pregnancy was my personal wake-up call, to begin to learn the rules for the game of life. I didn't feel ready to have a baby, so when my pregnancy was confirmed I broke down, cried and, in that moment, I was unsure of what to do next. Yet, having a child has forced me to grow in ways I didn't see coming, has given me the opportunity to stop racing through life and appreciate the moment. It also enabled me to build a strong foundation for my life, based on self-love, truth, awareness, strength, acceptance, trust in myself and faith all things are possible through the Creator.

I realised I had been sleeping on my purpose, getting sucked into a life of mediocrity instead of playing the game of life and expecting to win. The toughest moment in my life became the biggest blessing and opportunity to redesign my reality. What appeared at the time to be me hitting rock bottom gave me the opportunity to focus on the inner work and rebuild me in the way I believe God had planned.

*'I've learned that when you stay grounded in the truth of life's magnificence and your glorious divine power, all things become easier. Even better, an upward spiral of success and happiness will begin to lift off, gathering momentum to the point of you truly being unstoppable on your journey of self-discovery, revelation and love.'*

**~ Mike Dooley ~**

In this chapter, I will introduce you to three key ideas which have been monumental on my journey to rebuilding my foundation post-pregnancy. I trust the following principles will give you what you need according to where you are on your journey.

## The Mind is a Muscle, Build it Daily

What happens to your muscles after a reduction in exercise? Do you agree they become weaker? Just like any other muscle, the mind needs exercise to stay sharp and help you to get what you desire consistently. This becomes a struggle when we are not taking the time to build this muscle on a consistent basis through reading, visualisation, focus, journaling, creativity, listening to podcasts, writing down our goals, affirmations and study.

During my second year in business, I used to frequently slip into states of depression and, when I would finally surface and let my coach know what had being going on, one of her first questions would always be: 'Have you been doing what you know to do?' This meant going to the gym, which makes me feel alive, journaling, taking action and writing down what I am grateful for. Nope! Guilty! In my darker moments, that would be the last thing I would do, even though I knew building my mind muscle daily is the very thing that would keep me focused on the positive things in my life and out of depression. I can see the effects of taking your mind to gym daily, especially with one of my clients, Angela. I often know whether she has been doing her inner work or not, by how she shows up to our calls each week. You can build your mind muscle anywhere you like, anytime of day, which I believe is key to a transformation.

**What do you do daily to build your mind muscle?**

## Knowledge of Spiritual Law is Necessary

Three years ago, I became heavily focused on personal development, metaphysics and looking more closely at how our mind works. I recently came across Florence Scovel Shinn's work, which have become my go-to books for understanding and application of the principle that thoughts become things. If you are also focused on transforming your life for the better, I would encourage you to become familiar with her work. It is to the point and the instructions are clear.

*'Most people consider life a battle, but it is not a battle, it is a game. It is a game, however, which cannot be played successfully without the knowledge of spiritual law'*
**~ Florence Scovel Shinn ~**

The premise of this game of life is that what we think about, we can bring about. Therefore, it is important to learn to visualise the good which we wish to see manifested in our lives. Simple, yes, but the dysfunction that many are born into, including me, has kept individuals from discovering the basic truth that we are co-creators. We design our reality day by day through our thoughts, the words we speak, the stories we refuse to let go of and the beliefs given to us by others who also had no idea how to play the game.

I've coached many women who believe their experiences cause them to create new beliefs about the way the world works. However, the work we do together consists of going back to their past to see how it was their beliefs, wounds and childhood traumas that supported the creation of those experiences. I have learned that knowledge followed by application of spiritual law help us as human beings to live deliberately and purposefully, creating a new reality, one that we desire. You may be reading this and thinking: 'Get out of here Nofisa, life is hard'. But I want you to take a moment to think back to where you first heard that statement, and you will begin to realise what I am talking about. You didn't wake up one day and begin to feel this way; someone else believed life was hard and constantly reminded you of their belief until you adopted the same thought. From there, any experience that was hard simply strengthened your belief.

I have good news. A belief is simply an idea one thinks repeatedly, so we have the choice at any time to replace thoughts that do not serve us with ones that do. Knowledge of spiritual law helps us to know what is true in any situation we are confronted with, supporting us to see clearly where our thinking is flawed and needs correcting to experience a powerful shift in our reality. I believe the most challenging aspect is learning to let go of what I thought to be true and to live life according to law. However, it is most rewarding as I am beginning to see my life transform in an exciting way.

## By Our Words Our Reality is Set in Motion

*'By your words ye are justified and by your words ye are condemned. Many people have brought disaster into their lives through idle words'*

**~ Florence Scovel Shinn ~**

During a one-year mastermind programme with the amazing Joanna Turner, the ladies in the group had a saying which I too began to adopt. Whenever something negative was said we would quickly add 'cancel, clear, delete' to avoid creating a reality we did not want. I am a firm believer our words are powerful and we can speak both what we want and do not want into existence. A colleague told me the story of how her father and brother died relatively close to each other. Her brother became ill and the father declared, 'I will not be burying my son'. Her brother did eventually pass away, but not before his father, who became sick in a short space of time, dying before his son as he could not bear to bury him.

The above is not an isolated example. How many individuals do you know or have you previously been around who constantly say:

- 'I am broke'
- 'There are no good men out there'
- 'Life is hard'
- 'I am sick'
- 'I am not good enough'
- 'I am too old to...'
- 'I am a failure'

> 'You have built up a fixed idea that life is hard and filled with disappointments. You will meet these thoughts as concrete experiences in life, for out of the imagination are the issues of life'
>
> **~ Florence Scovel Shinn ~**

Look at how these individuals are living their lives. Is the use of idle words matching their reality? I am betting on yes. Many will say 'I call it how it is', but I have learned life will alter after a change in our thoughts and words, and not the other way around. I have recently got into the habit of saying 'I am tired'. However, those words are not supporting the feelings I want to create, so it is time for me to drop the negative 'I am' in favour of phrases such as 'I am energised', 'I am of great spirit', something along the lines of a positive statement. I am not saying you cannot be tired, sad, or be at a point in your life where money in your account may be low. However, what we focus on grows. It is therefore important to concentrate on what you want to experience, focusing your time and energy on that feeling, to bring about a change.

I know and appreciate we are all doing the best we can with what we have, however I believe we can learn to do better and it begins by being open and willing to change, as well as welcoming new ideas that may work better than our outdated ones. In the next section you will have the opportunity to create your own 'I am' statements. I know simply being aware of what you are saying and checking yourself each time is going to jumpstart a shift in the way you show up for life. Enjoy the process.

## LET US EXPLORE

Check yourself: Over the next twenty-four hours, observe yourself in your activities, your thoughts and words, then answer the following;

What 'I Am' statements do I repeatedly use?

_____

_____

_____

_____

_____

_____

_____

_____

_____

What 'I Am' statements could I deliberately use each day to support the reality I desire to create?

_____

_____

_____

_____

_____

_____

_____

_____

**What were my predominant thoughts today?**

_____

_____

_____

_____

_____

_____

_____

_____

_____

_____

_____

_____

_____

_____

_____

_____

**Did I take time today to build my mind muscle?**

- *If Yes... How did I feel as a result?*

_____

_____

_____

_____

_____

- *If No... What stopped me from creating the time for this today?*

_____

_____

_____

_____

_____

**Are the above answers supporting or hindering my ability to live my best life?** *(Be brutally honest with yourself)*

_____

_____

_____

_____

_____

_____

_____

_____

_____

_____

_____

_____

_____

# CHAPTER 2

# Life Lesson Two

## DO NOT PLAY VICTIM, TAKE 100% RESPONSIBILITY

*'When you're a powerful person you can't play victim... there is no
room in life to feel sorry for yourself, it's like, yo, let's go.'*

**~ Nicki Minaj ~**

This by far is one of the most game-changing lessons I have learned.
If we are to begin living our best lives and be the most powerful
version of ourselves, we need to take 100% responsibility in our
career, parenthood, business, relationships and so forth. Basically,
every day, we must own our shit:

- *Let go of blaming others*
- *Share our concerns with people who can help make changes to
issues we have*
- *Speak our truth*
- *Look to how we can alter our responses to achieve a desired outcome*

This can often be hard to do. I know it was for me and, in some
areas of my life, it still is, yet this is a powerful life lesson to adhere to.

A year after Jevon was born, I finally found the courage to end
what I had with his father. I was unhappy, and no longer felt I could
count on him to tell me the truth. I am sure he had his own issues

31

with me that were never communicated, so you can imagine the tension building up on both sides, with no healthy way to express what we were feeling and needing from one another. I knew in my gut that holding on to a relationship – or better yet, a situationship – for the sake of my child was not a smart move, so when he visited us in London for Jevon's first birthday, I made up my mind to end what we had.

During the two months after the split, I witnessed Jevon's father become less involved. Yes, it was slightly more challenging as I was in the UK and he was in the USA, however the Skype calls ended, the financial contributions dried up and I would only receive a text once every seven to ten days with the same line, 'Wat sup? How my son doing?'

I remember so clearly, a phone conversation I had with my son's father in January, 2014. On this day he declared he would be taking time out as a father for the next few years. He boldly told me our conversation would be the last until Jevon was aged three or four and could talk. In addition, he decided I could survive parenthood alone and announced he would no longer be helping me financially. Standing in my living room, with a fifteen-month-old baby hanging on to my legs, shock, frustration, anger and disbelief replaced the image of the cool, calm and collected woman who had begun the conversation. The salty tears returned and please believe I had a few choice words for him, but it did not change a thing. Begging him to think about his actions did not change a thing either; he had made up his mind and I was left on the other side of the phone like a lost little girl, feeling truly alone, afraid and unsure of what the future would hold for me as a single mum. I cried a lot that day and in the months leading up to the conversation. In fact, I cried so much I later found it had caused a blood vessel to burst in the back of my eye, leaving me scarred with mild distortion. Something had to change as I could no longer continue feeling and acting in this helpless way.

## Taking Responsibility

A few days later I woke up with a new zest for life and a strong desire to pull my big girl panties up and take full responsibility for the outcomes I experienced moving forward. I realised in that moment I had a choice...

Be disturbed by the choices he was making and blame him for the struggles of my life, telling everyone willing to listen to my drama how bad a person and father I felt he was (we all know misery loves company).

OR

Get a job, work on myself, focus on giving my son the best life I could, leave the door open for Jevon's father to re-enter his life in the future, discover my purpose and continue to move toward becoming the best version of me.

*'There is only one person responsible for the quality of life you live. That person is you... in short, you thought the thoughts, you created the feeling, you made the choice, you said the words, and that's why you are where you are now.'*

**~ Jack Canfield ~**

I soon learned, by signing up to a Jack Canfield coaching course and reading The Success Principles, that we call this taking 100% responsibility for our lives. You see, it is not about what happens to us that determines our outcome, it is about how we respond to those events. Had I chosen to meet his actions with a continuous negative response, I would have had an entirely different experience. This is not to say the choices he made were not upsetting but I refused to play the blame game. After all, nothing ever just happens to us.

- *It was I who made the choice to be with him*
- *It was I who ignored my intuition which told me to walk away when we began dating*
- *It was I who said yes to unprotected sex*

- *It was I who hoped he would be the father I wanted for my child*
- *It was I who refused to believe his words, when he shared how he would behave if we ever split*

## I Had a Feeling That...

Personal development has taught me to be aware we are always given warning and time to change our responses, which enables us to have an entirely different experience or prevent an unwanted outcome.

About three weeks before I became pregnant, right in front of me, my son's father was flirting with one of my colleagues and whispering into her ear (to make me jealous, he would later share). My intuition told me loud and clear to end things, as I knew I did not want to date someone who went out of their way to make me feel insecure. I paid attention and told him I no longer wanted to date, yet a mere week after cooling things off, lust and longing got the better of me and I was back in his arms without a clue my life was about to drastically change.

We often ignore these gut feelings, clues, comments or peculiar behaviours because paying attention to them would mean doing something different, potentially resulting in:

- *Unwanted change*
- *Being uncomfortable*
- *Being alone*
- *Confrontation*
- *A break-up*

For me, staying away would have left a feeling of loss I did not want to deal with back then. So I ignored the voice that whispered, 'You don't have much in common,' and his consistent attempts to make me jealous by sharing which famous women he wanted to sleep with. I ignored my intuition and witnessed the consequences.

In those moments, we get to choose how we respond. Playing the victim means reacting with a 'woe is me' response:

- *'There are no good men out there'*
- *'Every man is a heartbreaker'*
- *'I will never have a great relationship'*

Taking responsibility means reacting to situations by standing in your power and making statements such as:

- *'How would I do things differently in my next relationship?'*
- *'What do I need to change within me to avoid experiencing a similar situation again?'*
- *'How am I creating the outcome I am experiencing?'*

Remember, in every situation you get to choose how you will respond: play the victim or take responsibility.

# LET US EXPLORE

**Are you taking 100% responsibility for the outcomes you are experiencing in all areas of your life?**

_____

_____

_____

_____

**Are there any warning signs you are ignoring?**

_____

_____

_____

_____

**What needs to happen for you to change this situation?** _(No matter how uncomfortable)_

_____

_____

_____

**What are one to three actions you can take now, to begin to move toward a better outcome?**

1. _____

2. _____

3. _____

# Life Lesson Three

## BE WILLING TO CREATE PEACE WITH YOUR PAST

*'If we can identify the core of our struggles while simultaneously understanding we are truly in control of conquering them, then we can utterly change our trajectory.'*

**~ Rachel Hollis ~**

I was unaware when starting out in business and attempting to increase my income, one of the biggest steps would be to clear my past trauma, negative emotions, limiting beliefs in addition to dealing with the lies I had been telling myself over the years. I came to realise past experiences have shaped who both you and I are today, and if we are not awake to our truth, these experiences can keep us from living our best life, loving fully, making the money we desire, taking risks and so forth.

## Learning to Let it All Go

After Jevon was born I moved cities, away from my support system, which was around the same time his father cut contact. 'Alone' and 'unhappy' were the dominant emotions that washed over my body day after day until I got tired of feeling that way. I wanted out of the constant feelings of rage. Some days I focused on what life could've been like if I had never met this man and other days I was pure pissed at him. I was also pissed at myself because I was not living up to the woman I thought I could and should be; with so much ambition, I was playing small, yet had no idea what I needed to do to create a different reality.

One of the most common things I hear, when coaching and speaking to women about moving toward what they want, is they have no idea how to first move past their current pain and drama. Like I said above, I had no clue either until I realised, (through embarking on a journey of self-discovery and being willing to do whatever I needed to rid myself of pain and regret), that being tortured by unresolved anger and depression was damaging my soul and bringing more hurt into my life. This would always result in a barrage of repetitive experiences. I needed support to move past what I felt. I knew I could not do it alone and looked for support to discover my hidden blocks. It was not long before help arrived in the form of the talented Joanna Turner, also known as *'The Flow Alchemist'.*

It is okay to seek support to help move through painful emotions, experiences and heal old wounds. I knew a girl who, at my age, was married with one child and was beyond miserable, yet her husband refused to seek marriage counselling or therapy. Today I am not sure what has become of that family, but I know the last time contact was made, the wife was unhappy, yet chose to stay for the sake of the child, continuing to dismiss unresolved feelings and issues.

*'Feelings buried alive do not die, they corrupt and pollute the soul.'*
**~ Iyanla Vanzant ~**

In 2017, after sinking into what felt like my worst period of depression, I reached out to Joanna Turner. First and foremost, the cost of one year working with her was more than I was making at that time in my business as a coach, but something had to change, and after about thirty days spent trying to figure out how I would pay, I borrowed the first instalment and jumped right into my journey of clearing up my mess.

Our first session lasted almost four hours, and let me tell you straight, I cried constantly and my nose ran like a water fountain, leaving me looking like the hottest mess. But I came away feeling lighter and having compassion for friends and family I had felt were out to hurt me. We discussed how I had punished myself for getting pregnant and the feelings of both rejection and abandonment by my son's father, I held on to far too long. We also discussed my resentment toward my mother I refused to shake and how I struggled to accept her as she was, to healing negative feelings toward my friend Chanel, who had stopped speaking to me a few years before. We did not do much healing work on my feelings toward my father that day, and this is a relationship I am still highly triggered by. However, Rome was not built in a day, and healing years of pain and suppressed emotions often takes some time. Nevertheless, it was a profound experience that opened the way for me to continue doing my inner work, trusting I had the answers within. The best thing I learned from working with Joanna was that by changing my perspective and taking personal responsibility for every situation and experience I found myself in, I had the ability to forgive others and move toward being my best self, unapologetically.

In the first six weeks of working with Joanna, I experienced powerful changes from the inside out. My relationship with Jevon's father became easier and I began to make more money. I also became a much more powerful coach, supporting women to reach new levels of inner peace. All this became possible when I learned how to let go of emotions, beliefs and stories which were no longer serving me and instead chose to focus on the things I desired to create in my life.

# Healing Your Inner Child

*'It is very important to start awakening to the truth that there is nothing inherently wrong with our being; it is our relationship with our self and with life that is dysfunctional. And that relationship was formed in early childhood.'*

**~ Robert Burney ~**

Revisiting your childhood can be uncomfortable, yet this is a process I encourage to set yourself free. I am doing this work for my own healing and growth, but there are many adults who continue to allow their inner child to run their lives and are ignorant of this fact. So I am doing this for them as well, so they can be free to be who they are, today.

The pain and shame an innocent young child felt when being inappropriately touched by someone who was supposed to be responsible for her does not simply go away with time. But as an adult, an unwillingness to own the emotion and experience may lead to trust issues, self-loathing, depression, addictions, co-dependent and dysfunctional relationships. This ordeal must be healed. The relationship you have with yourself today is what is creating your experiences and your reality, and if you do not like the results you are getting, you can change them. But first you must identify the causes, most of which occurred in early childhood.

After watching *Whitney* and hearing her life story in detail, I have drawn a personal conclusion. I believe a lot of the troubles she faced in adulthood stemmed from trauma and unhealed wounds, many which were likely created during her childhood experiences, such as the alleged sexual abuse from a family member. I am not concluding this is the only reason for her troubled years, addictions and untimely death. But I believe had she learned to heal her little girl and find who she truly was instead of playing a role everyone else needed her to play, Whitney Houston may have been able to find her way out of the darkness, back into the light, and remain there instead of being a victim, self-sabotaging until the end.

I have worked with women who have endured emotional, physical and sexual abuse, experiences no individual wants to go through, yet Robert Burney explains, 'it is necessary to own and honour the child we were to love the person we are'. Imagine a world where we are no longer laying blame for what happened to us; where the lies do not exist; those lies we were told as a kid by individuals who were fed the same B.S. stories and had their own problems. These same people perpetuated a cycle and they likely had no idea how to overcome it. But you have the power to break it, to prevent history from repeating itself and creating further dysfunction.

The first step is to simply become aware. Become like a detective interested in investigating the causes and effects of your experiences. It may sound crazy, but I have so much fun and interest in this activity. I love to uncover the reasons why I created certain experiences in my life, such as attracting unavailable men and consistently sabotaging myself when it came to success and money. Awareness is power, as from this stance you can make a choice to continue down the same path and experience similar results or do the work to heal and move forward, loving who you are.

## Do Not Be Afraid to Do This Work

It was a Sunday evening and I got on the phone with a young woman who wanted a complimentary coaching session. The lady informed me she almost cancelled our call as she was unsure what to expect and did not think a visit to the painful past was going to be good for her. Yet there she was, ready to go at the designated time. Turns out, the young woman was holding on to a lot of baggage including anger, pain and feelings of abandonment over the death of her partner a few years before.

During our call, I took her through an exercise designed to help an individual have a heart to heart with someone's Higher Self, enabling them to begin to shift their perception on any given situation/experience, if they are willing, of course. This woman left our conversation feeling released, and able to better explain the reasons for her thinking or acting in a certain way. It was uncomfortable for her; there were tears, yet the woman who left that phone conversation was more aware and in a better position to make choices that would support her to move in the direction of her goals.

*'You cannot heal what you won't speak.'*

**~ Iyanla Vanzant ~**

I also recall another fearful woman who wanted to work with me, yet in the end her fear won over and she pulled out after paying a deposit. What makes this individual stand out is that after saying a big fat **yes** to working with me, despite her hesitation about doing the inner work, she immediately smashed her iPhone screen. Now that to me screams fear of paying to change her life, fear of getting uncomfortable, fear of looking at herself, so energetically she created drama to sabotage her efforts. I explained to her what was going on, but she was not ready to commit to the process. One thing I know for sure is that one must be willing and completely available to receive the healing.

**Are you ready to begin to create peace with your past to move toward creating the life you were destined for?**

# LET US EXPLORE

*'Our woundedness is not the sum total of who and what we are.'*
~ **Katherine Woodward Thomas** ~

## THE LETTER...

Writing down what you feel can be extremely powerful. Write a letter to someone you are finally ready to forgive. Taking responsibility for your actions and role in creating the situation. Let the individual know:

- *Why you are ready and willing to create peace with your past*

- *What you have learned through the experience(s)*

- *How you have grown through all you have gone through*

- *Your biggest lesson*

- *The blessing that can be found in the situation*

- *That you forgive them and are letting go of the hurt that has passed between you*

Once your letter is complete, you can burn it, tear it up, shred it, or send it to the person; the choice is yours.

# CHAPTER 4

# Life Lesson Four

## TRUST YOUR INTUITION

*'Intuition is our unerring guide. Practise following it in little things, then you will trust it in big things.'*

**~ Florence Scovel Shinn ~**

As I expand my knowledge of universal law, diving deeper into the teachings of metaphysics and energy healing, I often catch myself looking up, laughing and saying, 'Thank you universe' for the blessings and help I receive daily. Small coincidences such as someone offering a ride when I most need it, an offer to babysit without being asked, support from an individual which helps move me closer to a personal goal, receiving a cheque in the post when I most need the money, or reading something that instantaneously helps me feel better about the situation I am in – things like this occur and I think to myself, the universe really does have our back. I have learned that by paying more attention to thoughts, feelings and what is happening in every moment, I become more in tune to life's magic. Saying thank you is simply one way of telling the universe you are wide awake to your good.

## First, You Must Listen

*'Prayer is telephoning to God and intuition is God*
*telephoning to you.'*

**~ Florence Scovel Shinn ~**

We must learn to listen and trust our intuition is guiding us to the very things and lifestyle we have asked for. If you are reading this chapter thinking, *'Nofisa, I get what you are saying but I do not know how to listen to my intuition or trust that it will steer me in the right direction,'* I get it, I really do. Most of us were never taught how, myself included. I have taken the time to gain knowledge of spiritual law and have had to develop the skill of quieting the chatter within and listening to that small voice or gut feeling which peacefully points me to the right path.

Ever said to yourself, 'I knew that was going to happen'? Yes, you knew because your intuition spoke to you. But the question is, did you listen or ignore it? I've ignored my intuition on a few occasions, whether out of fear, denial or to make someone else happy, and let me tell you, it always ends badly. As a young woman, when I did listen to my intuition I had family members who would become upset because I chose to do what I felt was right for me, not what they thought was best. If you have also had this experience, this may have led you to trust and place other people's ideas and opinions above your own, creating unwanted experiences and a disconnection from what you know to be right for you. Florence Scovel Shinn has been my biggest mentor on the journey to learning to trust my intuition. I have read her books repeatedly, which has allowed me to lean on my faith and be still even when everything around me is going crazy. I highly recommend you plunge into her books sooner rather than later, beginning with *The Magic Path of Intuition.*

# What Are You Being Guided to Do Next?

*'Intuition is a spiritual faculty that does not explain but simply points the way.'*

**~ Florence Scovel Shinn ~**

Around January 2017, I began to feel a strong urge to spend some time in California in September that year. More specifically, I was being led to the city of San Diego, but I had no idea why. I just knew I had to be there in September, so I booked a flight. A few months later when I began the year-long coaching programme with Joanna Turner, it just so happened San Diego was to be the location of the next three-day mastermind, you guessed it, in September. During that time, I received the breakthroughs I needed to move forward in my life and business because I dared to follow my hunch. One of my breakthroughs was moving through the pain of struggling to love myself and own my beauty as a teenager and young adult: it was a powerful experience and I may not have been present had I not trusted my intuition and cleared my schedule for the trip.

## Our Gut Feeling is Enough to Act

I can honestly say I have not once been guided down the wrong path by listening to my intuition. Sometimes we may have a hunch but refuse to act without proof what we feel is the right thing to do or say. I realised this during a visit to the USA when Jevon was just four months young. My hunch became a sickening feeling that would not leave. My heart beat faster when he was near, and every fibre of my body told me he was up to something messy, so I went looking for proof and it did not take long to find. One message thread revealed all I needed to know; he had been meeting up with another girl from work and, when confronted, he denied everything until he realised I already knew the truth.

I am going to be real and say I needed proof to justify why I ended things, for others more than I needed it for myself. I was not confident in who I was and what I felt at the time, so I needed a tangible reason to break things off and explain my reasons without family members looking at me like I was crazy. Today, I would not give two fucks about what others think of my decision to walk away from a situation I am unhappy in, which highlights my growth and the confidence I have developed over the last six years. Hindsight has taught me you do not need to wait for proof. Go forward fearlessly trusting your hunches and asking for a definite lead when you are unclear of the next step. Then pay attention as your lead may come in any form, for example a conversation with a friend, something you read, a passing remark from a stranger, a symbol or a hunch to do something. However, it will come, let me assure you. If you ask, you shall receive. You are powerful beyond words; never underestimate that power.

# LET US EXPLORE

Start listening to your intuition and journal what happens when you follow it. Also, journal the consequences of not following it. You can do this daily, for a week or commit to it for thirty days

**What was my experience of paying attention to my intuition?**

_____

_____

_____

_____

_____

_____

**What were the signs I received?**

_____

_____

_____

_____

_____

_____

**What happened when I listened to my intuition?**

_____

_____

_____

_____

_____

_____

_____

_____

**What was the result of ignoring my intuition?**

_____

_____

_____

_____

_____

_____

_____

**How can I ensure I listen to my intuition consistently moving forward?**

_____

_____

_____

_____

_____

_____

_____

# CHAPTER 5

# Life Lesson Five

## THOUGHTS AND WORDS BECOME THE REALITY THAT IS YOUR LIFE

*'The imagination has been called "The Scissors of The Mind" and it is ever cutting, day by day, the pictures man sees there, and sooner or later he meets his own creations in his outer world.'*

**~ Florence Scovel Shinn ~**

No truer words have been spoken than those Florence Scovel Shinn uses above. Sooner or later you will meet the creations of your mind in your outer world (if your thoughts do not change). There is one creation that was so powerful for me, I was afraid if I told the story people would think I was crazy. That, however, was before I began to accept the principle 'thoughts become things'.

It was a weekday afternoon and I was taking a nap after my early morning shift with Virgin Atlantic Airlines. This nap was like no other. As I lay there sleeping I saw him, a baby boy wrapped in a white sheet resting peacefully in my arms. A familiar face was there too; however, he was standing further away from us and I was not speaking to or able to touch him, yet he was there, that was clear. One of the managers at Virgin Atlantic was also present, informing me that due to having a baby I could no longer work for the airline.

I was then instructed to go back to London. It felt so real. I woke up feeling hot and pretty shook up by the dream, but what really freaked me out was that Jevon's father had called my phone while I was asleep because he had been missing having me around. This would have been normal, but we had not spoken for a week as I no longer wanted us to play the dating game. I must admit I missed something about him too; maybe his presence which I had become used to in a short time, so I allowed him back into my life. Unknowingly, I was setting the stage for what had played out in my dream.

This was not the first or last time I had images of a young boy flash across my consciousness. While in the USA, I would often see vivid pictures of me travelling through an airport with a little boy, always just the two of us. I simply did not realise what I had visualised would soon happen in my outer world, a reality I was not ready for, yet something I was clearly thinking about at a subconscious level.

Everything played out pretty much as I had seen in the dream that day. I gave birth to a baby boy the same year and it made me laugh when the doctor asked, 'Do you want to know what you are having?' To which I responded confidently, 'I already know it's a boy'.

The distance between my son's father and me in the dream I believe was the physical followed by emotional distance between us once I left New Jersey. The only difference between what I dreamed and what became my reality was that I was not sent back to London by my job, because I chose to keep my pregnancy a secret and finish my contract. I left New Jersey to return to London when I was five-and-a-half months pregnant, after ripping every work skirt to accommodate my growing belly and wearing a blazer even in the sweltering Jersey summer days. My manager did say to me once, 'You know if you were to tell me you were pregnant I would have to send you back to the UK.' That was enough to keep me quiet, as I was not ready to head home and deal with a disappointed father and brother, who stopped speaking to me after I broke the news of my pregnancy.

The two principles – what we think and what we speak of – give us great power and become our reality. I believe that no matter your current circumstances, you can start from today to begin thinking differently, which in turn will begin to produce the positive results you crave. We are always creating our reality; the only issue for those who are not yet where they desire to be or who have not seen the results they hope for is that they are focused and thinking about the wrong things. Any of these thoughts sound familiar?

- *'I am afraid I am going to be alone'*
- *'I fear that it will not work out'*
- *'I am so scared of getting sick'*
- *'I do not want to say the wrong thing and have everyone judge me'*
- *'I do not love myself'*
- *'I am afraid if I get into a relationship he will try to break me down''* *(This was me)*
- *'I have nothing exciting going on in my life'*

*'Resentment and intolerance rob man of his power. We should have signs in the subways and shops – Watch your thoughts! Watch your words!'*

**~ Florence Scovel Shinn ~**

This is in no way to make anyone feel bad for having these thoughts – I have fallen prey to most – but an opportunity to expose the negative thoughts for what they are. Whether you are aware of it or not, you are creating all the time according to what you are focused on the most. This is an invitation for you to begin focusing on ideas and beliefs that will produce the results you would like to see in your outer world.

*'You are an ancient spiritual being who not only chose to be here, but who is literally co-creating the stage you find yourself upon. Here, all things are possible and your thoughts literally become the things and events of your life.'*

**~ Mike Dooley ~**

## LET US EXPLORE

**What is one thing you truly desire?**

_____

_____

_____

_____

_____

_____

**Are there any thoughts, doubts or fears which may prevent you from manifesting that which you want? List them below.**

_____

_____

_____

_____

_____

_____

**What empowering statements, if focused upon consistently, would support you to manifest your above desire?** _(Use the statements below for inspiration)_

- _Through the Creator all things are possible_

- _I am a powerful individual and that which I want can be achieved when I focus, have faith and take consistent action_

- _I am worthy of all that I desire_

# CHAPTER 6

# Life Lesson Six

## NOBODY IS HOLDING YOU BACK EXCEPT YOURSELF

As I mentioned earlier, at age eighteen I stopped sitting on the sidelines and put myself in the game of life without much knowledge of spiritual law. I had a fierce desire to win and I accomplished every goal I set out to achieve over the next five years: driver's licence, college distinction, qualified fitness instructor, move to another city, first-class degree, and move to the USA. Have you ever felt unstoppable? That was the feeling I woke up with daily during my early twenties. I remember my niece's mum asking what I would do if I did not get the job in America after university; my response to her was, 'There is no plan B, that job is mine.' And so it was. I had success blinders on, and it felt so good. Momentum is magical. Having decided on what I wanted, nothing or nobody was going to get in my way. I simply was not counting on myself being the major obstacle to success.

## Be Aware of Your Upper Limit

*'The upper limit problem is the only problem we need to solve.'*

**~ Gay Hendricks ~**

I repeat, I was feeling so damn good in my life. Then, within a year of moving to America, I was back in the UK living with my mother, with no job, on government benefits, a new baby, a 'situationship' I was unhappy in, feeling stuck, and my confidence had hit rock bottom. How does one go from feeling awesome to awful? I like to call it self-sabotage at its finest; Gay Hendricks refers to this experience as hitting your upper limit. I had hit mine, and I had no idea how to transcend this limit I had unknowingly placed on myself. The only way was back down.

Have you ever experienced being truly happy in a relationship then thinking *can things really be this good?* So, you do something unkind such as create an argument to go back to that comfortable place of fighting, sadness and feeling alone? One of my good friends, Sonia, is facing her upper limit and we can both see clearly how she is sabotaging her relationship. The man she is dating adores her; he is kind, will drive miles to see Sonia, offers to pay for everything, and tells her often how beautiful she is. This can be scary for many women, including me, and especially women who have not allowed or attracted this type of man/level of treatment before. Sonia often creates arguments with her new guy and pushes him away as she is scared he will eventually do this to her. Our job is to learn the tools and skills necessary to receive with open arms that which we desire, instead of doing just about anything to get rid of it.

My upper limit rears its ugly head most often within the areas of success and money. Up until now, whenever I had been at a place where I was winning consistently and moving forward, I had always created a way to sabotage my efforts. Most recently I would go as far as to sink into depression. My thinking was *if I did not feel good, there was no way I could show up consistently and put positivity out to the world.* This also comes from a core belief of not being good enough, a belief I have had to work hard to let go of in order to move toward all I am seeking.

The issue for most is ignorance. If one has no idea they are facing an upper limit problem, they will not take the steps or seek the help needed to move past it. It was not until I hired a coach that all my sabotaging behaviour came to light. I firmly believe once we know better, we can then make a choice to learn how to do better. You do not know until you know.

The second issue is one of worthiness. We must know with all our senses we are deserving of all we seek and give ourselves permission to have that which is meant for us, including good health, abundance, great relationships and peace of mind. Transcending our upper limit requires us to have an awareness of the behaviour we are displaying and a willingness to go within to change our beliefs, redefine who we believe ourselves to be and learn to love the perfectly imperfect person both you and I are.

## Are You Tired of Yourself Yet?

*'The life you are living is far below your God-given talent.'*
**~ Steve Harvey ~**

Sometimes we must get to a place of being so tired of our own bullshit that we force ourselves to make the necessary changes. I got tired of blaming my lack of success on being a single mother and decided to do whatever was necessary to move forward. What are you tired of in your life?

- *Procrastination*
- *Attracting unavailable men*
- *Always being late*
- *Blaming others*
- *Blaming yourself*
- *Comparing yourself to others*
- *Self-doubt*

- *Lack of confidence*
- *Fear of taking risks*
- *Allowing drama to consume your thoughts*
- *Toxic relationships*
- *Being lazy*
- *Being unorganised*

The above behaviours will keep us stuck and away from sharing our gifts with the world. The biggest way to hold yourself back is to think you do not have enough time and money to achieve your heart's desires. Again, this is the bullshit story you will continue to tell yourself to keep from living your best life. How do I know? I have made the same excuses far too many times, until I had both time (way too much on my hands) and more money and still failed to get the results I craved. It was only then that I swallowed the truth pill, looked at how I perceived myself, the stories/beliefs I held about who I was, and what was possible, and finally realised I had major self-love and healing work to do.

I was completing a series of questions about success recently and one exercise asked the reader to write down three obstacles to getting what they most desired. I thought long and hard. The things I want to do, be and have are completely within reach and possible for me with practise, focus, personal development, authenticity and refusing to quit before the win. Therefore, my response was me, myself and I, for there is nothing stopping me or you from starting today to move toward what we truly want. Each one of us has the power to begin right now, from where we are, and simply take the next step on this journey. Therefore, we must be willing to do whatever it takes, beginning with giving ourselves permission to live the life we envision and being vigilant against the ego's attempt to keep us from our greatness and the life we were born to have.

# LET US EXPLORE

If we are the only ones holding ourselves back from our good, we also hold the power to create a new reality. Think of the ways (and areas of your life) you may be holding yourself back and answer the following;

**What is it about me that has caused the situation I am in now?**

_____

_____

_____

_____

_____

_____

_____

_____

**Are there any fears I have about experiencing a new normal?**
(Dig deep to uncover your fears about unleashing your full potential)

_____

_____

_____

_____

_____

_____

_____

What am I willing to do differently to experience a new normal?

_____

_____

_____

_____

_____

_____

## Feedback from Others

Over the next seven days, ask three to five people the following question;

*'How do you see me holding myself back?'*

Using the table below, write down their feedback and create a plan to begin moving yourself forward

| Person Who Provided Feedback | How I am Holding Myself Back | How I Plan to Move Forward |
|---|---|---|
|  |  |  |
|  |  |  |
|  |  |  |
|  |  |  |
|  |  |  |

# PART TWO

# Life Lessons
# on Love, Sex and Magic

One of the most common questions I get asked by men and women is *'why are you single?'* I would often respond with a shrug followed by a silly comment about not meeting the right one yet. But I am keeping it 100% real with you; that comment is not my truth. Like many women, I have had a rollercoaster ride in relationships and decided to take myself out of the game of love because I was afraid I would lose and be left heartbroken.

In my head, focusing on building an empire and becoming the best version of myself left no room for broken hearts or new wounds, so I spent the last twelve years withholding love and holding on to very strong beliefs a relationship would interfere with achieving my dreams. *'Oh, but what if your guy supports you to get to your goals, helping you to move forward faster?'* a coach once asked. I had never thought about being supported and loved on the way up, and assumed that having achieved my desired level of success, my ideal man would be waiting for me at the top. The stories we tell ourselves, and the power we give to fear, is bewildering.

*'Your task is not to seek for love, but merely to seek and find all the barriers within yourself that you have built against it. It is not necessary to seek for what is true, but it is necessary to seek for what is false. Every illusion is one of fear, whatever form it takes.'*

### ~ A Course in Miracles ~

I was unaware throughout my twenties that my relationships and the guys I was attracting were simply a reflection of the relationship I was having with myself. The fears. The feelings of being unworthy. Old wounds manifested in my world as unavailable guys, men who were afraid of commitment and men who attempted to put me down, which all fuelled my belief I should remain single and in control. However, by the age of 29 (yes, just a year ago), I finally got tired of ignoring the part of me that ached for companionship. I began the journey to removing the obstacles that had kept love away for so long, such as the beliefs I mentioned earlier, resentment toward the key men in my life, and previous experiences which left a fear of commitment embedded in my consciousness. I have now decided to take personal responsibility for attracting to me the kind of relationship I desire to have, instead of living in fear a relationship will destroy all I have and am yet to build.

As you dive into Part Two, remember I am the guru of my own life, and what I have learned may be exactly what you need to hear to receive your breakthrough – or it may not. Again, I invite you to take what is relevant to you and leave what you do not need, but if you are going to turn the page, I ask you simply keep an open mind.

# CHAPTER 7

# Life Lesson Seven

## FALL IN LOVE WITH YOURSELF FIRST

*'Clean up your relationship with you, first and foremost.'*
**~ Katherine Woodward Thomas ~**

Many of us grew up having little knowledge of how to truly love ourselves. Now is not the time for the blame game, it is simply what was then, but does not have to be what is now. As an adult you have the choice to take back your power and love every inch of the person looking back at you in the mirror, which is important as our relationships are simply a reflection of the relationship we have with ourselves. A hard pill to swallow? It was for me; first I was blind but now I can see. Let's go a little deeper.

Growing up, I felt as if it was a crime to love all of who I was. If I attempted to look good on a day when there was no party, I would hear remarks such as, 'Why are you all dressed up?' Is it not enough to want to feel and look good because I am alive and loving on me? Regular comments about my weight, skin and hair from my mother, father and elders did nothing to support the journey to loving myself, and instead took me down the road of self-loathing. I grew up feeling uncomfortable about who I was and how I looked. I was afraid of being judged instead of feeling proud as fuck to be Nofisa Caseman. That was a problem.

You are going to get tired of me saying this but repetition is the key; you have got to hear this enough times to know that intentional self-improvement, changing my life from the inside out, is the number one reason I have fallen madly in love with who I am, why my life has changed for the better, and FINALLY I have begun to attract high-quality men. It starts with you.

## Be Your Own Best Friend

*'If you want to be treasured, you have to treasure yourself first and then show someone how to treasure you.'*

**~ Regena Thomashauer ~**

Ever noticed the person who speaks the most trash about you is often your own inner critic? I noticed this and was determined to create a healthy environment on the inside because, without it, my attempts at experiencing a positive external environment were futile. I sometimes catch myself attempting to say mean and negative things, however the awareness alone helps me to quickly change the language to an affirming conversation.

My advice is to start noticing the way in which you speak to yourself. Is it with adoration, empathy, love and kindness, or with disrespect, put-downs and negativity? The more I acknowledge the greatness within, the more I realise how the people in my life are simply mirroring and treating me the way in which I treat and speak to myself. Be your best friend first and foremost and you will begin to attract a higher number of quality relationships. Also, your relationships will be transformed for the better and the toxic ones will miraculously begin to fall away.

## Experience the Magic of Self-Pleasure

No adult really spoke to me about sex, self-pleasure and intimacy growing up besides the weekly, hour-long sex-ed class we had in high school. I have no recollection of what was even discussed, I just remember sex being this uncomfortable subject people would shy away from. I even tried to find out what age my mother broke her virginity in the hope I could use that as a benchmark for my own experiences. But she refused to talk about anything of that nature while I was growing up, so I was left to pretty much figure it all out on my own with the help of online resources such as good ol' Google.

I often question how many other young females have had similar experiences and, as a result, what their views are today around the subject of sex and intimacy. The effects of not being able to talk openly about sex in a safe and loving environment can lead to years of shame and a life of feeling disconnected from our bodies, expecting others to please us yet never learning what it means to give pleasure to ourselves.

I felt it was only right to include this topic in the book. Allowing myself to explore the magic of intimately getting to know every inch of my anatomy has awakened me as a woman, and I now feel both connected to my body and confident. Before I continue, if talking about sex and intimacy is uncomfortable, I am not forcing you to read this section. Feel free to pass and go directly to the next chapter, or keep an open mind and continue reading. Remember, you get to choose.

*'Unless you own your sensuality, you will only be dependent or needy or desperate in your couplings. True partnership comes only after true ownership.'*

**~ Regena Thomashauer ~**

I grew up thinking I had to wait for someone else to please me, which is a lie, and I give thanks I was able to uncover the truth early in life. Myself and friends have connected with guys in the past because we felt we were missing out on feeling good, a lie we were living due to never being taught to master the art of self-pleasure or how to truly love all of who we were. We looked for love and pleasure outside ourselves first.

I distinctly remember telling friends more than once I hooked up with a guy I knew was no good for me because I was 'horny' and needed to feel pleasure, yet this individual was a selfish lover and not interested in pleasing me in the slightest.

That was the level of my self-esteem at one point. As I grew to understand and experience the pleasure I can give to myself, I was able to own my truth, which is *I do not have to rely on someone else to create bliss within my body.* I am not saying I do not need a partner, I am simply suggesting that, alone and together, you can create pure ecstasy by getting to intimately know your zones of pleasure.

'Where do I start?' I hear those who have never ventured to this territory alone ask. You begin with no judgement and a willingness to discover the magic you already possess. Set time aside for your new venture and begin to explore your body with your hands, paying close attention to what feels good and not so good. Take time to enjoy you; give yourself a sensual massage or relax in a warm bath and explore your honey pot. Also, consider investing in the book *Extended Massive Orgasm: How You Can Give & Receive Intense Sexual Pleasure by Drs Vera and Steve Bodansky.* Just remember, this is your journey and you can take it as slow or as fast as you like.

*'The instruction manual for a clitoris reads: Educate yourself about me. Observe, listen, explore, appreciate, investigate. If you love what I, the clitoris, am feeling, I will feel more, and more, and more.'*

**~ Regena Thomashauer ~**

# LET US EXPLORE

*'Self-love is the only weight-loss aid that really works in the long run.'*

**~ Jenny Craig ~**

I thank Katherine Woodward Thomas for the following exercise, which I love. I have used it with coaching clients and the results were outstanding. I saw a massive shift, especially in my client Rachel, who began to love on herself so much more, embracing and accepting her current body while working toward the body she desired.

If you find you are judging specific body parts, use the following exercise daily until you no longer feel the need to criticise, judge or shame your body.

1. **Undress and stand in front of your mirror, hands by your side, and take some deep breaths.**

2. **Start at the top and work your way down your body, noticing any judgements you have with an area.**

3. **For each body part you are judging (e.g. stomach/thighs), do the following three steps:**

   - *Ask this part of your body to forgive you for judging, not accepting and being critical toward it.*

   - *Tell this part of your body something you love and appreciate about it.*

   - *Say thank you to this part of your body for something.*

**Record Your Thoughts, Feelings and Breakthroughs Below.**

# CHAPTER 8

# Life Lesson Eight

## NEVER LOSE YOURSELF

*'A woman serves a man best when she has her JOY above all other values.'*

**~ Dr Victor Baranco ~**

I believe one of the hardest things to experience is losing yourself within a relationship. If you have ever felt lost or are feeling like you do not know who you are or what you want right now, I guarantee if you are willing to go back and dig, you will be able to identify the exact moment you began to stop doing the very things that make you the wonderful individual you are. That was the case for Dina, a newlywed who became a client.

Initially, Dina reached out to me through Facebook as she wanted clarity around her new business venture and support to lose weight. I offered Dina a ninety-minute complimentary coaching session and, in this time, it was evident there was more going on for her. After a year of being married, having hit depression, experiencing weight gain and completely lacking in self-confidence, for a newlywed, to me there was something off with this picture. It became apparent once Dina had moved in with her fiancé followed by their marriage, she had slowly begun to stop doing all the things that made her the woman she was before becoming a Mrs, and slipped into a dark period, unsure how to reconnect with her light. Exercise classes stopped, meetups with friends decreased and Dina's confidence dwindled. I knew exactly what she needed in that moment; a simple back-to-basics plan which focused on reigniting Dina's passions and helping her to regain her independence and self-confidence.

In a few weeks I began to see Dina transform, coming alive before my eyes. Why? Dina was doing her inner work; she was following my coaching and taking the steps to get back to what she loved to do, and it was working. This for me was a pleasure to witness.

## What is it You Love to Do?

I have seen too many women make the mistake of giving up their desires, not doing the activities that light them up and trying to give all their time and attention to the main person in their life. When we begin to give up all we once loved and that which makes us who we are, we begin to lose ourselves. We then look to our partner to fill that empty space or fill it with things that do not progress us as a woman, like negative thoughts, depression, insecurity and complaining.

*'If you allow your rhythm to be interrupted, you'll create a void. Then to replace what you give up, you'll start to expect and need more from your partner.'*

**~ Sherry Argov ~**

I recently caught myself slipping, so fast I had to snap back in record time before I completely lost a part of me to the game of lust. To illustrate how easy it is to begin sacrificing what matters for the sake of being around someone, I offer this to you: I realised I needed to regain control of myself after I cancelled a hair appointment, missed a session with a mentor and was late for a few other personal appointments, just to hang out with a guy who, quite frankly, I had no business being with at that time. This may sound like nothing, but that is how it begins; a cancelled appointment here and there, a missed date with friends in favour of hanging out with your partner or a special someone, until eventually you find you have lost your independence. I never let it get that far, but have you ever found yourself in that situation? It is important to keep doing the things that light you up. Enjoy time as an individual as well as a couple and do not make sacrificing what is important to you a habit.

**This is How You Maintain Your B.I.T.C.H. Status
(Babe in Total Control of Herself)**

# LET US EXPLORE

What are the activities you love to do? Take five minutes now to write down a list of up to ten (or more) activities that light you up.

1. _____
2. _____
3. _____
4. _____
5. _____
6. _____
7. _____
8. _____
9. _____
10. _____

Make a commitment to yourself to keep these pleasurable activities alive and look back to this list if you ever feel disconnected. You may notice you have stopped doing what lights you up.

# CHAPTER 9

# Life Lesson Nine

## NEVER BECOME THE OPTION
### (Remain the Priority)

This by far has been the most difficult part of the book to write as I am going (and growing) through this experience as I type.

## In the Beginning

It took a while to hit me but, when it did, the feelings came fast, hard and strong. I could not remember a time I ever felt so comfortable, free and at ease around a guy; this one had me in my feelings like no other before, and the craziest part was I did not seem to care that he knew. In fact, I wanted him to know how much I appreciated everything he did for me and how his kindness put a smile on my face. His supportive nature was a turn-on and the way he looked at me; oh boy, let's just say was enough to create waves of pleasure within every inch of my body. In the earlier days I thought to myself I could not possibly handle his touch, yet the first time he embraced me, I hoped he would hold on tighter and never let go. I was in deep, I craved him, I wanted him to be 'the one', and that was a problem.

You see I never intended to grow feelings for someone I could not be with; that must be one of the most difficult situations to get yourself into. Nevertheless, I slowly found myself becoming more attached to the 'unavailable guy'. He was not married, he did not call it a relationship and they no longer slept together (he told me), but none of that mattered. Whichever way he chose to look at his situation, the individual I was growing deeper feelings for still lived with the mother of his child. Major fucks!

I wanted to be with this guy; I had never met someone who made me feel so freaking good just by being present. He had the qualities I longed for in a partner; caring, affectionate, a good listener and a gentleman. I felt like a Queen in his presence. Yet we could never be together while he was in that situation. My core values would not allow it. Regardless, lust and longing were beginning to take me prisoner and the struggle to break free was becoming a long and arduous process. I was at risk of becoming the option and not the priority.

## How You Become the Option

He hated when I used the word 'side chick' in his company, yet if I carried on down the road I was going – wanting to talk on the phone, enjoying activities together, buying each other things – I felt this is exactly what I would be to him, as his living situation had yet to change. I had to face it; he was still entangled with another woman and little things such as visiting my family home on Christmas day with her belongings laid out in his car often reminded me of this uncomfortable fact.

You become the option when you begin to accept things as they are, allowing yourself to get caught up in the triangle or love affair, instead of demanding that until the situation changes, you will not invest energy into that relationship, risk doing something that makes you feel bad about yourself or threatens your values. When we begin to accept less than what we know we deserve, we enter the world of accommodating another person. This is exactly what I began to do.

Despite him thinking he was an available guy and treating me as if I was the only one that mattered, I realised I would always be the option (and be kept at a distance) until he got his shit together. I also felt he would have strung me along (with the hope of an exclusive relationship) for as long as possible while continuing to coast. That is of course if I continued to be available for him to do so. In response to his words and actions, my emotions were up, then down and all over the place, like the scariest rollercoaster. It was a sight as I struggled between knowing I deserved more than he could give then, yet wanting whatever he was offering. When I was with him, he made me feel good, comfortable and safe to the point I refused to see sense long enough to walk away and stay away from the drama. I became my own worst enemy, ignoring boundaries, disrespecting myself and losing control of my emotions. Gradually I became weaker to his words and he slowly got more of what he desired from me.

Then I saw something I hated. It was the most terrible sight and made me sick. He did not need to rush to change his situation. It no longer felt like he tried hard to do right, so he could have exactly what he said he wanted... me.

Why was that?

I had caved in and given him the very things he craved. My loving, my time, my kisses, focus and energy, much of it became his for the taking, and he knew it. In that instant, it hit me hard. My whole body hurt with the realisation that I, Nofisa Caseman, had become the option.

Triple fucks.

## His Actions Will Tell You Everything You Need to Know

People can talk a good game but, let's face it, words only get you so far. Eventually someone is going to need to make a move, and if nothing changes or their promises continue to be broken, the answer to your unspoken question is in his actions, or lack thereof.

He told me I would be his soon and he was 'trying' to sort out his situation. He felt it was harder to leave the home they shared because there was a child involved. Yet one does not need to try; you either change your situation or you do not.

There comes a point when actions alone can tell you whether you remain an option or become the priority. Janet came to me for coaching last year. She was frustrated, angry and hurt. After seven years of broken promises, lies and living uncomfortably as the side chick, sacrificing her pride, values and self-worth, the married man she loved refused to stay true to his word and leave his wife so they could be together. Janet had met this man when his daughter was thirteen. He told her he did not want to break up the family until the girl was an adult, yet when the girl reached nineteen, Janet found herself still clinging to his broken promises and a man yet to be divorced. Janet was the option and, regardless of what the man told her, he clearly let Janet know this through his actions. She was not ready to hear and acknowledge the truth, so she held on tighter. After our coaching, Janet knew she could no longer entertain this situation and decided to end things as they were.

## What Can You Learn from the Situation?

If you find yourself facing similar circumstances and can relate to either mine or Janet's story, my first suggestion would be to focus on yourself. You see, you have the power; the only reason you are an option is because you have allowed it to be that way. It was a hard pill for me to swallow too, but it is the cold truth. If you do not allow it, he would be forced to change his situation and then pursue you or move on to the next woman who does not mind being 'the option'.

Take some time to journal on what your experience is trying to teach you

- *Are you showing up for yourself?*
- *Are you afraid of commitment?*
- *Are you in control of your emotions or are they controlling you?*
- *Do you fear being alone, so settle for less than you deserve?*

- *What do you need to let go of to allow unconditional love with an available person to occur?*
- *Are you clear on the type of man you want to attract?*
- *Do you know what you want?*
- *What will you accept in a relationship?*
- *Have you created boundaries?*
- *Can you stand by your word?*

As I sat with these questions, it became apparent I was still shit-scared of facing heartbreak. Due to my hidden fears around relationships, I kept attracting unavailable guys. Although with each encounter I was getting clearer and closer to the type of man I wanted, looking back there was still so much fear. Men who seemed like a great catch were always just out of reach. This way, to avoid being hurt, I could easily detach when it became too intense. What was happening was simply a result of what was going on within and, if I desired a different result, I needed to change instead of solely expecting the man in my life at any given time to make the changes. Once I changed within, my experiences would also be different. That change included getting and standing by a set of standards and letting go of old beliefs around relationships that no longer served me.

## Hindsight Has Taught Me

Let me be clear. In such a short space of time, what grew between the two of us was so intense I did not know how to deal with the emotions aroused. Frustration, anger, confusion, resentment, lust, adoration and impatience took over my body all at once and messed with my head. When I was with him, I was lost in his vision of what could be. When I was away from him, I constantly fought myself, knowing I needed to walk away yet finding it excruciatingly painful to let go and let God do what was best.

I was beginning to get mad at myself for my lack of control, and annoyed at this guy because I was allowing him to have that kind of hold over me. No matter how many times I told him to stay away, to let me be while he was dealing with his situation, we always found a way to be closer to each other. I realised I was losing myself to someone who at the time could not openly reciprocate the feelings I had and be the man I desired in my life.

My mentor told me to get out of the situation before I got too deep, but lust had already wrapped me tightly in its chains and I struggled to break free. I had repeatedly disrespected myself and broken promises by running back to his arms when I said I would not. This situation has taught me to…

## Create a List of Non-Negotiables

I have never created a list before. I guess it was standard that I was not the type of woman that would ever be labelled a home wrecker, but what about the blurred lines? What about my standards and values? What if someone wanted to be with me while he was still living with his ex? It did not feel good, but it was not a non-negotiable when we first connected, which is what really fucked me up. Moving forward, I have created a list of my non-negotiables, which are rules for my life I do not need to argue with, they just are. I highly recommend you create your own list.

## Create and Stand By My Boundaries

It is important you are clear about what you will and will not allow in your relationships. I broke personal boundaries and I was the one who ended up hurt and angry. Boundaries let the other person know you are serious about what you say, inviting them to change their circumstances/approach if you are the one they truly desire. A word of caution; if you do the opposite to what you say, it will encourage others to act in the same way. You must respect your own boundaries if you want others to do the same. He began to stop taking me seriously, when it was clear I was ignoring the very boundaries I had put in place. He would tell me to my face, 'I watch what you do and never really listen to what you say'. Learn from my mistakes; our actions do the talking, so check yourself.

**Side Note:** *A support network is needed for this step as there will be times when all you want to do is give in to temptation. But think of the long game. What is the outcome you truly desire? Act accordingly.*

## Never Ever Forget the Game

*'When a man approaches you, he has a plan and the main plan is to sleep with you, or to find out what it takes to sleep with you.'*

**~ Steve Harvey ~**

I forgot there was a game. Period. In the beginning, he admitted he knew just what to say to me as he would listen attentively and then respond in ways he knew I would love. But was that who he really was, or was it the character he played while attempting to access the main benefits?

I believe at some point getting what he wanted (even if that meant hurting me in the process) became the most important thing. He even told me '…breaking promises to yourself is OK', when I shared my frustration of once again finding myself in his arms after expressing the need to keep my distance. What a bunch of B.S! My emotions were temporarily off the leash. The whole situation had me fucked up, but breaking promises to myself was never OK. Continuing down the road we were on would only see one person lose… me. I started to see how quickly I was falling into a place I would have to drag myself out of alone. I had to get it together and refrain from giving him the benefits of being with me while he was still deep in his mess and could not commit. I did not announce my intention because that seemed to only intensify his mission. I simply created a list of non-negotiables, decided on my requirements for a relationship and began to fiercely work on me.

I have learned when we give someone everything they want in the beginning, because they have said all the right things that open the solid doors to our heart, we may end up losing because, frankly, you gave away freely everything they needed to make the right moves and win. Instead of telling a man exactly what you want, tell him what you require; this way you do not hand over the key to your heart but allow him to find and open it. To remain a priority, give yourself the gift of time before you give heavily of yourself, to find out his true intentions, if his actions are consistent with his words and to learn whether he can be the person you require and truly want in your life.

## Do Not Get Attached to the Outcome

I believe I found it harder to walk away when he was living with his ex, because I held on to the story he was the perfect guy for me. The best one I have ever met, so I clung to the hope of one day entering an exclusive relationship with him even though he was unavailable. Yet there is always a lesson beneath the chaos. Looking back, this man was a door opener (as one of my mentors likes to call it). He opened the door and showed me what a high-quality man looks like, which I had yet to experience. He also demonstrated to me what it felt like to be cared for. A great man indeed, but I realised I was attempting to force things to go my way, which was not in my best interest. I had to surrender and trust that if a relationship was meant to happen, a way would be made as I refused to settle for things as they were. In the meantime, I had to fall back and not mess with the universe's way of delivering to me the things I had asked for.

This is not to say the man in front of me, and potentially you right now, cannot be 'the one'. However, it is up to you to decide on the type of relationship you want and if he can meet your requirements.

If he cannot, have total faith there is someone who can and will be there for you like you envision.

## Get on With Life While He Handles His Business

He told me to be patient as things were about to change. I said I would wait for a little time but not forever. Logic slapped me on the back of the head and made me realise there was no need to put my life on hold while he dealt with his present situation and figured out his next step. I reduced contact with him so that I could keep a clear head and focus on me. I also continued to date other men while getting clearer on the qualities and experiences I wished to have with my ideal partner.

## Communicate

Eventually he moved out of the home he lived in with his ex. What I respect about him is how he openly shared where his head was at. This man was not ready for a committed relationship (I finally was), which allowed me to deal with things as they were and not as I wished or hoped them to be. His truth gave me the strength I finally needed to walk away. Regardless, I am forever grateful for the powerful lessons I received through this experience.

*'...find your voice to ask for what you want. Everybody has the right to tell you no or yes, but you always have the right to ask'*

**~ Don Miguel Ruiz ~**

# A MAN'S THOUGHTS

There is no way I could end this chapter without giving you insight into one man's perspective on this subject. He has lived this situation and been the man telling his side chick he would leave his wife but did not because he was too comfortable. He knows the games; he played them like a master. So, without further ado, I want to introduce you to Kendall Ficklin, mentor, author, speaker and entrepreneur. Go on Kendall, speak life into these women.

## Just Because He is Touching You Does Not Mean He is Feeling You

If he is in an unhappy place at home, he is likely to begin to look elsewhere to get his needs met. Be aware that just because you two are intimate does not mean he is going to leave his family, wife or other half to be with you. My advice: *'Let him get to know you before he gets to see you.'* What I mean by that is keep your clothes on and allow this 'unavailable man' to simply get to know you on a platonic level (*if you choose to stay around him in any way*).

## Kids Are Not an Excuse to Stay

Like the examples above, people will use their kids as an excuse to stay in a comfortable environment or avoid breaking up their family. The truth is, if you are unhappy in a relationship, staying for the children can cause more harm than good, so these lines people talk about not being able to leave their situation because of the children is simply not true. If someone feeds you those lines, the question is... What are you going to do?

## It's Either You Are Done or You Are Not

Let's get real here; there is no trying to sort out the situation. It is either he is done or he is not done. If the person you desire to be with tells you they are trying to sort out their situation, interpret that as *'I am not ready to give up this environment I am used to'* for whatever fear, stories or beliefs they have. The way I see it, if you are done, if you are unhappy in a relationship, if you have found someone you truly want to be with, you are going to be making the steps to move forward right now. You move out of the family house or you offer to help the other person find a place if there are kids involved. If there are no kids involved, it is like, *'Yo, what are you still holding on for?'*

My advice to any woman who has been told to be patient and wait for someone to leave their situation is, *'Walk away and let them sort it out in their own time, not on yours'.*

## Girl, You Gotta Walk Away

If you find yourself growing feelings for an 'unavailable guy', you are spending too much energy on someone who, right now, cannot commit 100% to you for whatever reasons. What you need to be doing is investing that time into building yourself up, getting your finances in order, loving yourself, working out, eating healthily and getting your mind right. That is what will allow you to be your best self. From that place, you are going to attract a great relationship. Walk away from the bullshit. To be the man for you, the man you are growing feelings for has some work to do in his own life. Most women will stay in the drama and become broken or hurt in the process. Do not be like 95% of women; walk away and know that what is meant for you cannot be lost. It will happen at the right time, when you are truly ready.

**Kendall Ficklin**

# LET US EXPLORE

If you have found yourself attracting a guy who, for whatever reason, is not able to make you a priority, answer honestly the following questions:

The reason I chose to stay in this situation is... *(complete the sentence)*

_____

_____

_____

_____

_____

_____

It is easy to disrespect and dishonour myself by staying with this person because... *(complete the sentence)*

_____

_____

_____

_____

_____

_____

I am afraid of... *(complete the sentence)*

_____

_____

_____

_____

_____

_____

**What story am I consistently telling myself that helps me to stay?**

_____

_____

_____

_____

_____

**What lessons can I take from the situation?**

_____

_____

_____

_____

_____

**What are the qualities I love in this person?**

_____

_____

_____

_____

_____

**What is it I do not like about this person?**

_____

_____

_____

_____

_____

_____

_____

**What do I desire to experience in my ideal relationship?**

_____

_____

_____

_____

_____

_____

_____

**How can I use this experience to learn more about myself?**

_____

_____

_____

_____

_____

_____

_____

_____

**What can I now focus on to bring me closer to what I truly desire?**

_____

_____

_____

_____

_____

_____

_____

**What are my non-negotiables for dating/relationships?** *(The Rules)*

1. _____
2. _____
3. _____
4. _____
5. _____
6. _____
7. _____
8. _____
9. _____
10. _____

They say writing things down helps to clear the mind and ease the soul. Writing poetry helps me to gain clarity around a specific experience and to clearly express how I am feeling. The following poem was written at the height of the emotional tug of war with the guy I refer to in *'Life Lesson Nine'*.

## 'ALL THAT COULD BE'

When I'm with you it's like nothing in the world matters but us
You've given me faith in what a relationship can be, and in you
I know I can trust
It's like none of this is important because I can't be with you
Yet I still impatiently await the day that you tell me you two
are through


What the fuck are these feelings I cannot run away from
Holding on to hope that one day I'll be yours, it's like I'm in a
motherfucking sitcom
I never intended to grow deep feelings for an unavailable one, the
way you touch and caress my body
These types of emotions I struggle to walk away from


I act as if it doesn't bother me that every night you go back
Don't ever get it twisted of course I feel a type of way, I just learned
to handle situations with tact
Hanging on to hope, this shit is nothing but a joke. Sometimes
I feel as though all you think about is yourself, playing me like a
toy and when you are done I go right back to the shelf
Now, I can either laugh or I could cry, but still I wish these feelings
for you would just die

Yet, I must thank you for opening my eyes to what a gentleman
should be, you are pretty fucking awesome it's like you walked into
my life with a key...
To open me up to love, I admit I was closed to the idea of giving
away my heart
Afraid every man would try to hurt me; I have felt the need to
protect myself by playing the game of love real smart

It's worked up until now because with you I don't want to do
that; if you were free, I wouldn't feel the need to run, close my
heart or hide
I would truly enjoy being the woman by your side
I get it, I'm living a fantasy and I am not here to force you to
join my reality, I just wish you would stay away while you deal
with your shit
Because let's keep it real you are an unavailable man and at
present cannot commit

Nor am I here to be your little secret, don't tell me any different
because that's what I am
Yet I've invited you into my world, ignoring the voices and signs
that say fall back until he's available, it's
like I don't give a damn

Seeing her things in your car that day made it all real
It doesn't matter that you say it's over, that's not what I feel
It doesn't seem as though you are taking big enough steps to move
your situation along
It really feels like you are coasting and bringing me for the fucking
ride in the back, which is wrong

You are the epitome of a great man; you deserve nothing
but the best
Yet I'm only hurting myself, by staying in this mess
It appears to me that you think by not talking about her and acting
as if she doesn't exist
You will just make all your problems go away and with me you can
have real bliss
But it's not real and I won't play this game any longer
I need a man who can fully love me and together we can build
something stronger

I'm going to make this really easy for you
I've decided that it's about time to walk away
Yeah I know I've tried and failed but if you respect and want the
best for me, do not try to convince me to stay

So this is my goodbye for now, I'm not saying it will be forever
But until you break free from your current ties in no way can we
be together
I think it's crazy how it is over before it ever really started
But I'm definitely not trying to be the woman that is left
broken-hearted
This has taken a lot of my energy, but I don't regret a second of
what we shared
Because I am now fully open to the idea of a relationship, when
before you I never really cared

So Mr, a massive thank you, now it is time I refocus on me
To follow my goals and dreams instead of staying focused on all
that 'could be'

# CHAPTER 10

# Life Lesson Ten

## FORGIVENESS WILL SET YOU FREE

*'Forgiveness is the choice to see people as they are now... By bringing the past into the present, we create a future just like the past. By letting the past go we make room for miracles.'*

**~ Marianne Williamson ~**

Before we begin this chapter, stop now and ask yourself, *'Is there anyone I need to forgive?'*

Take a piece of paper and write down the names of people you have yet to forgive, taking it back as far as you can remember, acknowledging what you were hurt about and how the situation made you feel (keep this sheet or sheets of paper safe as you will need them toward the end of this chapter).

I remember doing this exercise and being upset about things that happened when I was seven, which I still felt pissed off about as a grown woman, and that presented a problem. Remember, we cannot heal what we refuse to recognise, so take some time now to simply sit, think and write. I was unaware how deep my resentment for individuals such as my son's father, my mother and father went until I was invited to acknowledge my pain and agree I was ready to move forward without it. Only then could the forgiveness work begin.

The forgiveness process may be uncomfortable, it may feel like you are bringing up emotions you do not want to deal with. However...

*'...when you know how to forgive, you eliminate excess mental and emotional weight that keeps you stuck in repetitive situations, circumstances and experiences that are not healthy or productive.'*

**~ Iyanla Vanzant ~**

You may also feel that by forgiving others, you are agreeing with the behaviour displayed or the hurt that has passed between you and another, that is not true. But you would not be alone in your thinking, as I too held on to this belief way too long. I did not know how to forgive until I started in business and realised holding on to resentment was blocking my good and damaging my soul. It was keeping me stuck, so forgiveness and healing work became essential to setting myself free from the emotions that kept me in bondage, disrupted my spirit and left me feeling broken, wounded and accepting less in life than I deserved.

*'The other thing I am totally convinced of is that while forgiveness ain't easy, it's the most important inner work you can do within your mind and heart.'*

**~ Iyanla Vanzant ~**

It was my twenty-sixth birthday and Ryan, a friend from high school, and I decided to travel to New York, Atlanta and New Jersey to celebrate. Arriving back into Newark Airport from a weekend in ATL, Fiorella, my Peruvian sister, offered to pick us up. As Ryan and I walked toward the exit to meet her, I saw a familiar face, someone I had known intimately, a person who had not communicated with Jevon and me in almost a year. It was Jevon's father. My heart skipped ten beats, my skin began to feel hot, and I froze as mixed emotions washed over me. Although he had completely shut us out, this man was still the father of my child, so I pushed my anger aside and sashayed toward him. As I got closer he looked up, slightly shocked, and I simply asked, 'What is really good?' I know, random, but that is all I could muster at the time, even though my ego wanted to curse him for what I felt was an immature reaction to us breaking up and him being far away from his child.

SILENCE

Anger slowly crept to the surface. 'By the way, your son is doing great!' I spat out.

SILENCE

The airport felt cold and my heart heavy. He would not speak a word to me. In fact I vividly remember him putting his head back down as if to say, 'Why are you even talking to me?' So I fought back tears as I walked away, shocked that someone I had a child with could be so mean. Ryan had seen the whole thing and asked if I was okay. 'I'm fine, it's nothing,' I lied, but deep down I resented him. I was angry, but to the world I smiled and shrugged off the behaviour as if it was nothing. *There were plenty of other single mums out there who have endured worse than I have and they are doing well,* I reasoned. So I continued to focus on my goals and bringing up a baby alone, ignoring the anger when his name was mentioned. I would soon come to learn that ignoring my negative feelings was detrimental to my emotional and physical health as well as my success journey.

Six or seven months passed before he would attempt to reach out to me. By this time Jevon's father had not seen or spoken to him in almost two years. He called via *WhatsApp* one night and soon after I viewed the missed call, it was evident he had then blocked me. By this time a girl would be furious, but instead I became numb. I accepted he was going to do mean things because I know hurt people will try to hurt other people. Hurt it did, but a voice inside kept reminding me to leave the door open for him to come back and be a father when he was ready. At the time I did not feel as though there was much else to do anyway.

## Why Forgive?

I was speaking to a friend recently, telling her that although my life is not perfect (is anyone's, though?) and my frustration is mounting around the fact I have yet to finish this book (initially scheduled to launch on my birthday, which is less than two weeks away), I feel at peace within myself. A large reason for this has been my ability to own and work through my feelings (even when the emotions are painful) and learning how to forgive others. Oh, there are layers to forgiveness, indeed, and it may take you a while to forgive particular individuals in your life, yet having the tools and skills to successfully master this practise allows one to create a better future. Iyanla Vanzant goes as far as to say that, 'The only true way to create a more loving, productive and fulfilling life is by forgiving the past'.

I needed to forgive my son's father and take my power back, as we only resent someone to the extent we feel they have taken our power. I did not know how to forgive; more importantly I did not want to as I thought that would make what he did okay, until I realised that was wrong. Forgiveness is about the individual. Joanna was the first coach to support me on a deeper level to forgive both my son's father and me for all that happened and all the pain that had passed between us. The day Joanna carried out a massive clearing session with me, I immediately felt lighter and soon our relationship shifted for the better.

**Are you willing to forgive those you feel have hurt you in the past or present?**

# LET US EXPLORE

Grab that list you made at the beginning of the chapter. If you didn't write down a list of names, go ahead and do it now. You may have convinced yourself you do not care about a particular situation, but listen up; to strut into your power and live with more peace and joy, you are going to need to get emotionally honest with yourself. Let me give you some examples to get started.

- *An ex-boyfriend who cheated on you (like really, he could not control his urges)*

- *Your parents who made fun of your weight (not even funny)*

- *Friends who did not include you in activities (how could they miss how awesome you are)*

- *A boss who passed you over for a promotion (huff)*

- *A fellow boss babe killing it in her business (lucky bitch)*

- *Family members who seemed to be jealous of you (blame your parents for having star quality genes)*

- *Your husband for not acknowledging all you do as a wife (that's not cool)*

- *Your kids for acting real spoilt (could you admit you kind of made them that way?)*

- *Your teachers who made you feel you would not amount to much (what do they know?)*

So now you have an idea of all the people and scenarios you must forgive; take the first person/situation and follow this exercise (questions adapted from Katherine Woodward Thomas's book *Calling In 'The One'* to begin to forgive and release these past hurts.

- *Why do I resent (name)?*
- *What can I take 100% responsibility for in that situation?*
- *How can I grow from this experience?*
- *What blessings have come from this experience?*
- *What lessons can I learn from this?*
- *What have I refused to accept about the situation?*
- *What do I need to let go of so the situation is complete, I can take my power back and be free to live life the way I really desire?*

**Forgiving the past does not happen overnight. However, becoming aware of the resentment you have been holding toward others for many years, (then doing the work to forgive and release these feelings) is a major step in the right direction.**

# CHAPTER 11

# Life Lesson Eleven

## LUST WILL MAKE YOU DO DUMB SHIT

'It doesn't feel the same.'

If you have heard these five words before, you know exactly what this chapter is about. If you still have no clue, let me jump right in and set the scene so you can understand the predicament I was in when I heard these five, life-altering, big belly-creating words.

It was February 4th, 2012, and I was sitting in my three-bedroomed, shared apartment in the heart of Newark, New Jersey, awaiting the arrival of my sexy, chocolate, six foot. Here is the thing; I was unsure what we were calling it. Jevon's father and I were in the awkward stage, where we had been dating for three months, explored almost every inch of each other's bodies, but had yet to commit to something more than casual dating. My horny twenty-three-year-old self was not so bothered about titles; I wanted what he was giving to me on a consistent basis. He had me and he knew it. Have you ever had that experience where you are so focused on someone else that you were slowly beginning to lose yourself? That was me.

I digress.

Let's get back to setting the scene. Soon after, he entered the apartment looking irresistible as ever in his uniform and black Nike ACGs. Before I knew it, he had me spread out on the single bed, I loved to watch him handle my body in a way no man had. Before intercourse, I ensured he had on protection.

Immediately he whispered, *'It doesn't feel the same.'*

Damnit! I knew what he meant, I did not need an explanation. I was so deep into feeling his body connect to mine that saying no was not an option I wanted to consider as, in that moment, he was my drug and I was ready to get high. Without thinking of the consequences, I bowed down to lust, allowing him to enter my honey pot again, but this time without protection.

You know the rest. Jevon was born nine months later, 6.10 lbs, cute as ever, and my life would never be the same again.

## Russian Roulette

I am sure many of us can admit to having unprotected sex. I remember at the age of fifteen travelling on two separate occasions with a friend to the sexual health clinic on Brixton Road, London, for her to request the emergency pill. I used to think to myself, *girl, you didn't learn your lesson the last time or the time before that, wrap it up, it cannot be that hard.* That was the virgin in me talking and it is clear to me now lust will make you do dumb shit. Period.

For example, I had not asked my son's father to get a sexually transmitted infection (STI) test before we got intimate, nor did I know much about his overall health. So not only did lust have me caught up, which ended in a pregnancy I was not ready for, I realised I was carelessly willing to risk my own health to satisfy my sexual desires. Luckily for me I did not walk away with an STI, but those consequences were simply not playing on my mind in the heat of all the intimate moments we had together.

In life there are times when temptation will sweep over your body and engulf you in a false sense of security. Clearly ignorant, I did not expect to get pregnant. I know others have had similar thoughts and faced the consequences of their inability to properly protect themselves. I have also noticed over the years, many (including myself) believe the withdrawal method to be an effective way to avoid a pregnancy. However, having personally played the game of Russian roulette in the bedroom, I know it is a game you do not want to play with just anyone.

A while ago I read *The Wait*, written by DeVon Franklin and Meagan Good, which was a powerful wake-up call. After reading the book in a day, I decided to abstain from sex for a period, getting to know myself on a deeper level as well as avoiding a lot of the unnecessary drama that comes with having sex with someone before you really know them. Some of the reasons I chose to abstain were:

- *Removing the risk of STI or babies I am not ready for*
- *Not wasting time with someone I know is not a good fit for me*
- *Getting to know someone on a deeper level without sex clouding my judgement*
- *I want to know someone is with me for the right reasons and not solely how I make them feel between the sheets*
- *To focus on the potential the Creator has placed within me, knowing I will attract a great relationship in divine time*

I invite you to read *The Wait*. Whether you choose to abstain from sex or not, there are some gems in this book which can support you to re-evaluate and change areas of your life for the better. Yes, lust can make you do things you said you would never do but, by practising the wait, I found the ability to stay in control of my experiences. There may be a weak moment, you may surrender to lust; my advice is to not beat yourself up. Remember, you can always continue to practise the wait, if you so choose to.

## The $5 Cookie Jar

My friend recently shared a post on Instagram which had the caption 'tag a friend who can relate', with a picture of a jar and a note that read, *'I said I wouldn't hook up with him then I did it again.*

*Jar – $5'.* I damn near cried with laughter because I can more than relate to that.

So, here is my challenge for you if lust continues to have you in a chokehold. Grab yourself a jar and write a note specific to your case; you can also use the note mentioned above. Once complete, place the jar somewhere you can see it daily. Any time you find yourself giving your power away by bowing to the very thing you said you would not do, throw a five (in your currency) in the jar.

Awareness is the first step to change, and seeing that money pile up will alert you to the fact there is more work to be done. But, if no money is going into that jar, you are standing strong. Celebrate yourself and continue to work on you, just keep the jar around to ensure you stay in control.

# LET US EXPLORE

Without a doubt, I allowed myself to be blinded by lust and fell pregnant by a man I barely knew. If you feel you may be with someone for the wrong reasons, take some time to journal on the following questions.

Would I still be with this person if sex were not involved?

_____

_____

_____

_____

_____

Can I see a future with this individual?

_____

_____

_____

_____

Am I repeating a negative pattern?

_____

_____

_____

_____

Can I be my true self in their presence?

_____

_____

_____

Can I become the best version of myself while with this person?

_____

_____

_____

Is this relationship/situation right for me at this moment in time or am I using it as an escape?

_____

_____

_____

What can I learn from this experience?

_____

_____

_____

My next step...

_____

_____

_____

# CHAPTER 12

# Life Lesson Twelve

## RELATIONSHIPS ARE THE CLASSROOMS OF LIFE

*'No man is your enemy, no man is your friend, every man is your teacher.'*

**~ Florence Scovel Shinn ~**

When we look to the issues in our relationships, we often focus on what the other person is doing (or not doing) and try to change their behaviour. It never occurred to me – that is, until I began to work on my man issues – that dating and relationships are powerful opportunities for our own personal and spiritual growth. They help us forgive others, love selflessly and learn to love ourselves, create healthy boundaries, heal our own childhood wounds and relinquish the negative ego.

In her book *Return to Love*, Marianne Williamson says, '...relationships are assignments', a statement with which I wholeheartedly agree. It is time to pay attention. Our relationships or lack of a relationship can point us to the areas within ourselves that need to develop or have yet to be healed. People who are sent into our lives can be our most powerful teachers if, of course, you are ready for the lesson. If not, you will repeatedly experience similar situations.

## Why Do I Attract...?

Ever thought to yourself *why do I always attract men who cheat, don't want to commit, have baby mama drama, want to put me down, or are unavailable and incapable of loving me?* Oh, let me tell you, it hit me like a ton of bricks when I began to understand I was attracting the very experiences I did not want. You see, we attract what is inside us. What we are experiencing in our relationships/dating life is a result of our energy, thoughts, feelings, focus and words. If you are manifesting what you do not want repeatedly, i.e. an emotionally abusive guy, it is important to understand something within you needs to shift to experience a new reality instead of blaming your situation on something outside of yourself.

## What Do You Need to Learn?

More than a year ago, I joined an eight-week course to support my journey to attracting high-quality men into my life. Love coach Nicole Moore knows her shit and supports women across the world, to get amazing results in love and relationships. I saw a powerful transformation in myself by taking her course and, as she predicted, the men I began to attract changed for the better. That was all down to my mindset, thoughts and energy shifting first. I was open to doing the inner work (to a certain degree) and as a result my outer world reflected the changes I had made. It was exciting.

Yet, as I began to attract men into my life that more closely represented the individual I desired to be with, I still noticed I was, at times, attracting unavailable men. They were unavailable emotionally (because they were just getting out of a relationship) or physically (they were living with the mother of their child, even though the relationship had broken down). *What was inside me which caused an attraction to unavailable men?* I often wondered. It was not until I began to develop deep feelings for the man I spoke of in *Life*

*Lesson Nine*, that I dared take a deeper look at myself as the cause of my disheartening experiences.

Fear, worry, doubt and a scared little girl emerged from a deep dive into what was going on within. I wanted love, I desired to be in a relationship, but there was a part of me that was terrified to fully give myself to someone, to love with every fibre in my body, in case I got hurt. That allowed me to see there were still parts within myself that I had yet to heal and which were causing these experiences. Regardless, I did not want to keep running from love; I wanted to experience the magic, the good times, the times that test a couple, the challenges and joy with someone I could call my partner and best friend.

> '*Let us be fearless, then, in examining ourselves as the cause of that which is happening in our lives, so that the possibility of love is thereby restored.*'
>
> **~ Katherine Woodward Thomas ~**

## Clear the Space for Love

I have recently decided to kick my relationship fears and doubts to the kerb and allow myself the opportunity to love fully when the time comes. Following Nicole Moore's love coaching method, one of the first steps to begin attracting a high-quality man you desire to be with is to energetically, emotionally and often physically clear the space for love.

- *Do you need to get rid of photos and old jewellery from your exes? Now is the perfect time to make some quick cash*
- *Do you need to heal from your childhood wounds? Maybe you are unaware you are reacting from these past traumas*
- *Do you need to clear away fears and negative beliefs that keep you in repetitive situations?*

107

- *Does your home reflect space for a man or does it say, 'ain't nobody got time for that'?*
- *Does your calendar have space for dates or nights out with that special person?*

## What Needs to Shift Within You?

This may be a new idea for you, but the quicker you can grasp the concept that you create your reality and then take responsibility for attracting to you the relationships and experiences you want, the more in control of your future you will feel. This applies to not only this area of life, but for creating whatever you want. If we are not getting the results we want, we need to do something differently and not wait for our outside environment to change. A commitment to raising your level of self-awareness so effective change can take place will also be required. My advice is to consider hiring a coach, therapist, or perhaps seek out a spiritual advisor to support you along this journey.

# LET US EXPLORE

Go back to your journal and answer the following questions honestly. Take the time to reflect on your answers, highlighting where you can begin to make immediate changes for the better.

What results am I experiencing repeatedly in my relationships?

_____

_____

_____

_____

_____

_____

_____

_____

What am I doing/not doing to create this experience?

_____

_____

_____

_____

_____

_____

_____

_____

**What am I ready to let go of to develop my capacity to love?**

_____

_____

_____

_____

_____

_____

_____

**What needs to happen/what steps must I take to let go of the above?**

_____

_____

_____

_____

_____

_____

**Below are a few coaches I follow online who share quality content on the subject of relationships;**

- _Nicole Moore_
- _Matthew Hussey_
- _Iyanla Vanzant_
- _Trent Shelton_
- _Katherine Woodward Thomas_

# PART THREE

# Life Lessons
# on Career, Hustle and Flow

*'People often say to me "treat my business". I say no, I will treat you,*
*for you are your business.'*

**~ Florence Scovel Shinn ~**

For a long time, I have known that life as an entrepreneur is the ultimate goal for me; what I did not anticipate was how powerful, challenging and life-changing it would be, and I am only just getting started. In the beginning, I was ignorant when it came to business and did not have a clue about what it really took to succeed. The craziest part is I expected results to come as fast as I could click my damn fingers, which is exactly the reason I quit my job as a receptionist in 2015 to begin building an empire – *or so I thought.*

The first days were fun. I could sleep later, go to the gym and enjoy some me time when Jevon was at day-care. The best freaking part was having nobody telling me what to do, looking at the time I showed up at work or attempting to micro-manage me. I was officially my own BOSS. Boom! Nevertheless, the months to follow were tough and seriously lonely. I had no direction, no goals, no money, no focus, no mentor, no clear idea, no solid plan. Not much but a desire for a freedom-based lifestyle and a passion for helping other women to develop confidence and achieve their goals while I did the same in my own life.

I soon learned the life of an entrepreneur was not to be taken lightly; it would require me to do things I had never done and become someone I had never been. I knew that badass chick was somewhere inside of me awaiting the day I would completely set her free, but that could not be actualised as the woman I was then. My wounds ran too deep and my mindset was underdeveloped. There was work to be done, yet I had no idea where to begin. I was and remain a determined, resilient woman, yet in the first year of quitting my job, my self-esteem began to waiver, my bank account began to weep and I became disheartened as I struggled to break free from the shackles of my ego.

As the end of 2015 approached, I made a decision that would change the course of my life. I said the biggest YES to my own personal development by signing up for a one-year transformational coaching course at the grand total of $16,500. Sweat, nervousness, excitement and fear took over my body all at the same time as I sent the first payment and prepared myself to embark on a new journey. But let's back-up for a minute, as I do not want you to think I sent the first payment easily. Oh, no. Truth is, I did not even have that type of money in my bank account, like ever, but somehow I knew it was the right decision and the money would come. Following my intuition, I stepped into 2016 ready for what was ahead.

In this section, you will explore the powerful lessons I have learned by starting and failing in business, and doing whatever it takes to turn my desires into reality. 'If you want the best personal development course on the planet, then start your own business,' one of my mentors would always say. I second that, so pick up that journal and let's get to work.

# CHAPTER 13

# Life Lesson Thirteen

## START WHERE YOU ARE. START BEFORE YOU ARE READY. HECK, JUST START NOW

*'Every pro was once an amateur. Every expert was once a beginner.*
*So, dream big. And start now.'*

**~ Robin Sharma ~**

At the ripe age of 29, I can finally say I am giving myself permission to start where I am and stay in my own damn lane because I have seen first-hand what is possible if, like Dori from Finding Nemo says, you 'just keep swimming'.

Starting where you are can feel daunting, especially when you have not personally witnessed individuals start from the bottom and successfully move toward all they desire. I see the result of so many go-getters who achieve a high level of success, but I have never seen first-hand the whole journey up close and personal. In the past, I have been afraid of what others would think if they saw me putting in all the effort without much result at the start, but as I write this I am thinking about all the time and energy I wasted on caring about what the hell anyone thought about my grind.

People will always have an opinion, but you do not have to pay that any mind. If you are focused and determined to win, the ones who are on a similar path, I hope, are showing you nothing but love. Of course there will be a handful who see you as competition and will stop supporting you, which I have experienced. Again, you 'just keep swimming'. The ones who are not taking responsibility for creating the life they say they want… well, you are taking action and they are not, so nothing else needs to be said here.

## It is Always Awkward Before it is Elegant

A mentor once said, 'It is going to be awkward before it is elegant,' and that is because every master was once an amateur. There is a learning curve we simply cannot avoid if we desire to improve our skills, and we must have faith and trust that if we keep learning and practise, we will get better at the thing we wish to master.

One of my biggest fears when I first began to coach and speak to groups was, 'what if they ask me a question and I don't know the answer?' I was so afraid of looking like I was not good at what I was doing, yet that was my truth. I was not great at speaking or coaching; I had only just begun the journey. I also was not doing the work necessary to get better, instead trying to wing each speaking gig and coaching session as opposed to mastering my craft, a recipe for disaster.

I can still remember one of my first coaching sessions and how awkward it was. The lady was resistant to what I was saying, and it felt like I was pissing her right off. However, as a novice, I was not prepared to handle situations like that, and I wished the ground would swallow me up. I could not get off the phone quick enough. At another speaking gig, I walked into the room like I meant business; one of the guys in the audience was so excited to see me talk until I got on the stage and, in the first few minutes, mixed up my thoughts and forgot what I came to preach about. I had not prepared, because I had become used to individuals tooting my horn about my skills and fierceness on stage; I just felt like I had it in the bag. BIG MISTAKE, but lesson learned.

Fortunately I redeemed myself when, a year later, I hosted my own event, *The Fierce Female Live*, and blew myself away with the level of growth that was clear from how I showed up. Calm, in control, knowledgeable and cool when one of my speakers dropped out an hour before the show. I had handed it over to God and asked to be used through my work to support the women in the way they needed; it felt easy, natural and I felt blessed to be in that situation.

## Give Yourself Permission to Get Started

*'Fail early, fail often, fail forward.'*
**~ Will Smith ~**

One of the biggest reasons I feel many people never get started is the fear of being seen as silly or like they do not know what they are doing. Would you agree? As a pole dance instructor, do you know how many women I have come across that tell me how much they would love to try working the pole but do not think they would be good at it? I am like, 'Earth to woman, how would you be good at dancing on a pole if you have never been on one before?' Can you see now how crazy this thinking is? I recently tried network marketing and spoke with many individuals who refused to join because they believed they would be no good at selling, which of course most will not be if they have never done it. This is the reason for training, coaching, learning, application, and trial and error. Nobody is expecting you to be an expert before you have dedicated time to something you desire to do, so give yourself permission to simply get started, now!

I often feel like I have been raised in a society where people fear trying, failure and getting things wrong, but we must be the generation to end the madness. I tell my son when he is learning something new, 'I want you to make mistakes and get it wrong.' The quicker he does get it wrong, the more he will learn about what does not work. He will also see that it is okay to make mistakes. It is in the trying, failing and practising that a skill is developed or a problem is solved. I am helping him to learn to ride a bike and he is so afraid of falling. This may sound mean, but I told him the quicker he falls the easier it will be to teach him. Right now, my son is so afraid of falling that he cannot focus on riding. Once he falls and sees he is still okay, he can put his energy into fearlessly taking on riding a bike. He will know he can get back up after a fall and keep getting better until he masters it. The same goes for any endeavour, especially starting a business.

In closing, the biggest lesson is: start where you are and be willing to put in the time, energy and effort to practise and become great at what you truly desire to do. They say it takes approximately 10,000 hours to master something, and whether that is true or not, the quicker you get started in the direction you want to go, the better your world will be.

# LET US EXPLORE

*'Just decide, right now, today, that you aren't going to wait any longer, and that you're worth whatever it is you're seeking.'*
**~ Melinda Parrish ~**

## Redefine Success and Focus Upon the Small Wins

Instead of feeling like you have not made progress and your end goal is miles away, I invite you to make a list of what you consider 'small wins' in the direction of your goal(s). By focusing on what you have achieved instead of what you have not, you are more likely to stay committed, enjoy the process and believe what you want is possible as you move closer to its manifestation.

For example, when I first had the idea for writing this book, it felt like it was never going to be achieved. The project felt too big, but I needed to get started. So instead, I took small steps and held myself accountable for taking daily action toward my end goal. When it comes to writing a book, the main thing is to write every day, and as I did my writing became fluid and this book began to take form. Below are some of the small wins that enabled me to start exactly where I was and keep the momentum:

- *Write daily*
- *Complete a chapter*
- *Source a designer*
- *Have a photoshoot*
- *Get a front cover designed*
- *Source locations for launch*
- *Complete a blurb*

**What is your major goal for the next ninety days?**

_____

_____

_____

_____

_____

_____

_____

_____

**Write down all the steps you can take to move toward this goal**
_(Every time you take an action toward this goal, consider it a small win)_

_____

_____

_____

_____

_____

_____

_____

_____

**From the above list, choose one action you can take in the next twenty-four hours to start right now toward achieving this goal**

_____

_____

# CHAPTER 14

# Life Lesson Fourteen

## YOU CANNOT ESCAPE THE GRIND

A big fat realisation hit me back in 2015 when I quit my job to become self-employed. I thought to myself, *Damn, Nofisa, you really don't know how to grind*; my hustle was weak and I am fully owning it. I woke up in the mornings and was not taking on the world the way I had imagined I would. When working a job I disliked, I used to sit at my desk and daydream about all I would do, but when my dream to work for myself finally became a reality, I was paralysed. I spent most days in the house hiding, reading, over-analysing, overwhelmed, second guessing and procrastinating. I could have been out there creating content, writing articles, writing books, developing my coaching skills, sharing my journey using V-logs, networking and building my level of influence.

Although hindsight is always 20/20, it is never too late to begin putting this type of effort into building your dreams, as I am now beginning to do consistently. It was not that I was a lazy person; as with any goal, there is nothing that will stop me from moving forward with full speed until it is accomplished, that is if I truly desire to achieve it. In this period of my life, however, were a combination of things which held me back.

## Lack of Vision

*'Where there is no vision, there is no hope.'*

**~ George Washington Carver ~**

I had no vision. I knew where I was, but had no clear idea where I wanted to be. What did I want freedom to look like? What was I working toward? What did I want to be doing one year, five or even ten years from then? Can you answer these questions? Unfortunately, those are the questions I could not answer, and I never took time to sit down and journal on them.

'Your vision is a detailed description of where you want to get to,' says Jack Canfield. Life experience has taught me the value of creating a vision and, by getting crystal clear on what you want, the 'how' becomes a lot easier.

## No Plan or System to Follow

So now you may have your vision but, uh oh, you have no idea how to bring the powerful image you see to life. I have learned through being the girl with no clue that not knowing what to do is not an excuse to quit or take no action. If you have no plan or system to follow, your first goal should be to find somebody who is already doing what you wish to create and get the support you need to turn your dreams to reality. How did they get from where they were to where they are now? What were the steps? Observe, ask questions, learn, apply, analyse your results, tweak and repeat. The road to success leaves clues, so do not act clueless; now is the time to become resourceful.

A system is exactly what I found in the one-year transformational coaching course I joined run by multimillionaire Gina DeVee. Gina gave me a step-by-step guide to developing my coaching skills and building a business. It was an amazing year, and I can honestly say following the plan laid out for me, and dedicating my time to mastering coaching skills, resulted in paid clients before the year was complete.

It is the same with writing this book. I had no idea how to begin, so I reached out to Kendall Ficklin to be supported from start to finish. You do not ever have to do this journey alone, but you do have to make the first move. Whatever journey you are on, my advice would be to trust the process. Sometimes it will feel as though the results are not happening quickly enough, so quitting becomes an option. However, I now prefer to get to my destination a little later than planned, as opposed to never getting there at all. Think about that.

## Lack of Consistent Action

It is in the work and the grind that you will often find your answers. The more action you take, the clearer your journey will become, yet so many of us feel confused about our next step to the point of paralysis. I knew I wanted to coach women, yet I did not take much action on this goal in the first few months of working for myself, besides supporting a few friends to move forward.

A lack of consistency has been my biggest downfall. I have witnessed individuals start exactly where I began and reap the rewards of the seeds they sowed earlier simply because they kept grinding, refused to give up and took consistent action. All that you and I want is ours for the taking, yet without consistent action, which also includes consistent focus on what you truly desire, it will prove difficult to achieve results.

## No Mentorship

In the beginning I had no vision to pull me forward and no mentor to push me; when it came to business and making money, Lord knows I struggled to push myself back then. Around eighteen months after I walked away from the safety net of my full-time job, a gentleman reached out via Instagram offering to support and help take my business to the next level. Although I was getting results from Gina's programme, I confess, I wanted help to improve sales and visibility.

Kendall Ficklin, creator of *Grindation* and President of Eric Thomas Associates, taught me about The Grind. He could not have come into my life at a better time, and it quickly became apparent his methods of teaching were working. I even remember a friend of mine reaching out for his support because of my growth. Sometimes you need that father figure to keep it real, assist you to get out of your feelings and just work. Kendall helped me to book paid speaking gigs through nothing but personal reachouts, and supported me to build my following by delivering fire content.

I recently began working with Kendall again to get this book finished, and he is working his magic. Kendall has no time for my excuses, drama or reasons why I cannot get it finished. 'Just get the book done, that's all you need to do,' is his favourite line for me right now. So here I am at 10am on a Saturday, my son next to me watching cartoons, grinding for my dreams.

I believe you will find it challenging to move your business forward without the above. Please take the time to create a vision, follow a system that works (or create your own), take consistent action and learn from people who have already walked a similar path to the one you desire. Remember, we cannot escape the grind; the process is part of the package of a great life. All successful people grind to create the lives they have envisioned for themselves.

# LET US EXPLORE

Write your vision for your business, ideal career or another area of your life you desire to change for the better. Use the following questions as a prompt:

- *How much money do you make annually?*

- *What work are you doing daily? (Are you an entrepreneur or do you have your ideal job?)*

- *Who are you helping?*

- *If you could do one thing for the rest of your life and never get paid for it, what would you be doing?*

- *Are you living with purpose? (What does that look like?)*

- *Where are you located?*

- *How do you use your free time?*

Do not be afraid to dream big and create a powerful vision that will pull you forward. Just watch out for those dream stealers along the journey

*'There are people who will try to talk you out of your vision. They will tell you that you are crazy and that it can't be done.'*

**~ Jack Canfield ~**

Write down three new habits you will need to adopt to stay consistent and achieve your goals

1. _____

2. _____

3. _____

**To ensure you are consistently moving toward your vision, who will you recruit to hold you accountable?** *(Use the form below to contact a potential mentor/coach)*

| Coach/ Mentor Name | Date Contacted | Outcome of Conversation |
|---|---|---|
| | | |
| | | |
| | | |
| | | |
| | | |
| | | |
| | | |
| | | |
| | | |
| | | |
| | | |
| | | |

# CHAPTER 15

# Life Lesson Fifteen

## DO WHAT YOU GOT TO, UNTIL YOU CAN DO WHAT YOU DESIRE

The day I quit my full-time job, I swore I would never work a 9-5 ever again. I also expected the money to begin rolling in fast when I 'officially' began my coaching business. I had witnessed lots of online coaches sharing their stories of major success in such a short span of time, yet I do not recall them sharing their personal journey to getting to where they were in that moment. I had so many questions.

- *When did they first begin in business? (it was never six months prior, which we were led to believe)*
- *What were their daily habits?*
- *Did they ever feel like giving up?*
- *What did they have to sacrifice?*
- *At what point did they give up employment?*
- *How did they get started?*

Having insight into an individual's rise to success, the good the bad and the ugly, can be powerful because success leaves clues. You can see first-hand what that person had to do and who they needed to become to achieve all they have today. It is unfortunate many have not grown up with immediate family members who have gone on to become mega-successful, but that does not dictate what is possible for you. One of my mentors suggests reading biographies of the rich, famous and super-successful. These people explain the hustle and grind in detail, letting you know that if it is possible for them, there is no reason success is not possible for you, too. This is the reason I gravitated toward Kevin Hart's book, as he highlights exactly what he went through to enable him to do what he does today. The question we must all ask ourselves is, 'Are we willing to do whatever it takes to have what we desire?'

*'I was an overnight success, which took 16 years.'*

### ~ Kevin Hart ~
*I Can't Make This Up*

As I approach thirty, I have finally learned that sometimes you must do what you got to do, until you get to the place where you can do what you desire, on your terms. You see, when I first started in business, I was not thinking this way. I was working as a personal trainer, which I did not enjoy, so I moved to a different gym. I was much happier there with the variety of responsibilities as a fitness trainer instead. However, four months into the new gig, my ego got in the way and I decided I would soon be financially free, therefore did not have to work for anyone else. I could instead focus solely on building a business. I quit that job to give my all to becoming a coach. The issue was that I was a master self-saboteur, now without a consistent income each month to pay for my course and invest in my business. I also equated a low bank account with my self-worth for a long time, so when the money was low, my frequency was low, and I would take myself out of the game completely. I was not winning in business or life.

## What is Your Vehicle?

Building a business is a journey, and on that journey you may use several vehicles to arrive at your destination. As you get closer toward where you desire to be, your vehicle will be fancier, it will light you up and make you feel so damn good, but rarely does anyone begin driving in this. We often start in one we do not like, one that is uncomfortable, but we stay with it because we know it is helping us move toward our destination.

As I mentioned, this impatient lady, a.k.a. me, was not thinking like this when I started out. I saw being a coach as the destination and acted like I had already arrived, which was to my detriment. Having an appetite for travel and a desire to constantly develop myself required cash flow and lots of it. Quitting my job in the early days should not have been an option. I also did not have the work ethic to hustle 24/7 in my business, leaving me feeling in limbo and like things were stalling.

Struggle was the name of the game as the months went on. The course payments continued to be taken off multiple credit cards and my refusal to get a full-time job led to family members passing judgement and not taking the work I was doing seriously. I simply kept hoping (without applying massive action) that the next month would be the *the 5k month*'and all my money problems would begin to dissolve. Meanwhile, the credit card companies were beginning to dislike their late payments, and family members were frustrated about lending me money to support a dream they could not see coming to life quickly enough.

It took me three years to decide to go back to full-time employment that would financially support me while I was building my dream. It is not something I wanted to do and I felt ashamed, like I had failed in business. By then, however, I was beaten down by my lack of results. I just wanted to get back on my feet and start building my dreams from a place of feeling abundant, positive and excited about life.

A full-time job provided me with consistent income enabling me to begin rebuilding my business. Also, working full-time has allowed me to connect with a pool of talented individuals who have helped to bring this book project to life. Today I am working full-time and have multiple side-hustles, including teaching dance, coaching women one-to-one and speaking engagements. Revenue will also come from book sales once completed. The above is supporting me on the journey toward money and time freedom, and eventually I will put myself in a position where a large part of my day is filled only with the tasks and work that support my highest vision. Meanwhile, I have to do whatever it takes to move forward and be able to do the above.

I remember having a call with an individual – let's call her Tricia – who was interested in joining a network marketing business I was briefly part of. This woman had been thinking about leaving her job for more than two years. It became apparent very early Tricia wanted what success looked like but had no desire or intention to put the work in to get a specific result. With hindsight, I broke it down nicely. *'Tricia, you are kidding yourself if you truly believe you won't have to do much to create residual income. Do not let those Instagram pictures fool you. At some point you will need to put in work.'* Tricia was not prepared to do what she had to do, whether that was starting a network marketing business or creating another stream of income from her talents. It is sad to think, but I have a strong feeling to this day, Tricia is stuck in the same job she does not like.

## What is Your Why?

*'He who has a why can bear almost any how.'*
**~ Friedrich Nietzsche ~**

You have to have a strong why to withstand the journey to success. There will be challenges and obstacles; the universe will surely test your faith. Knowing why you do what you do will give you the strength to keep on going, especially when everything is telling you to give up. Having a strong why will also allow you to say no to the good so you have time and energy to say a big fat yes to the great.

My why is twofold: I am on a mission to support individuals as they get unstuck, develop self-confidence, and learn to love themselves so that ultimately, they can become their best self and attract into their life the things they truly desire. I have been in a dark place where I lost who I was, felt stuck and my confidence hit an all-time low. If I can move past this place by shifting my mindset, it is imperative that I help others to do the same. I also do what I do to create the life I envision for my son, myself and family. The more of us that are living with purpose, loving ourselves unapologetically and wanting to do our part to make the world a better place, the better the world will be. I hold on to my why and, no matter how often or how hard I fall, I will always get back up and continue the journey.

# LET US EXPLORE

Write thirty ways you can make money (your vehicle) to support your move toward the vision you shared in the previous chapter.

1. _____
_____

2. _____
_____

3. _____
_____

4. _____
_____

5. _____
_____

6. _____
_____

7. _____
_____

8. _____
_____

9. _____
_____

10. _____
_____

11. _____
_____

12. _____

_____

13. _____

_____

14. _____

_____

15. _____

_____

16. _____

_____

17. _____

_____

18. _____

_____

19. _____

_____

20. _____

_____

21. _____

_____

22. _____

_____

23. _____

_____

24. _____

_____

**25.** _____

_____

**26.** _____

_____

**27.** _____

_____

**28.** _____

_____

**29.** _____

_____

**30.** _____

_____

**What is your BIG, JUICY, why?** *(What is going to get you out there living with purpose sooner rather than later?)*

_____

_____

_____

_____

_____

_____

_____

_____

_____

_____

# CHAPTER 16

# Life Lesson Sixteen

## YOU DO NOT NEED TO KNOW THE 'HOW'

*'If you get clear on the what, the how will be taken care of.'*

**~ Jack Canfield ~**

'Know what you want and how it comes to you will be taken care of'. This is something I instinctively knew growing up. I never questioned the how, instead simply acting in the direction of my dreams while following my intuition.

This is something children do all the time. They live on faith, rarely questioning their own motives. They simply move with the flow of the universe and expect whatever they are doing to work. Note that word 'expect'. As we get older, we have that childlike faith drummed out of us because we are constantly subjected to the opinions and demands of the authority figures in our lives. We forget what instinct feels like.

When I started in business, suddenly I began a tirade of over-freaking-complicating things, which led to nothing but feeling stuck, often. By following this life lesson instead, you will begin to realise you do not have to do it all alone; there is a greater force working on your behalf to provide all you have asked for. You just need to get out of your own way long enough to work alongside the universe and not against it.

Before I proceed, there is one rule. You will need to trust the universe has your back. Can you do that?

*'It is not your job to make something happen – Universal Forces are in place for all of that. Your work is to simply determine what you want.'*

**~ Esther Hicks ~**

## How the Universe Has Worked for Me

When I was twenty, I created an 'I Want' list, which included flying first class and not paying for it by the time I turned twenty-five (super-random, I know). When creating the list, my imagination painted a picture of a corporate company paying for me to travel overseas to handle business. Although I got what I wanted, let me be clear it did not happen how I had envisioned.

Approximately five years after writing that list, I was travelling back from New Jersey via Virgin Atlantic Airlines and the flight was full, to the point they were looking for volunteers to catch the next flight 24 hours later. I was with my friend Ryan, but jumped at the chance to give up my seat because I knew it came with a free return ticket to any destination the airline travels to. Ryan was in a grumpy mood and refused to give up his seat, but I stayed, got my free ticket and came back the next day to return to London. As I checked in, the manager on duty said he had something special to give me, and I knew the universe had delivered. First class on Virgin Atlantic was happening that night, the thing I had asked for. And just three days after turning twenty-six.

Talk about the power of desire. I had my demonstration because I believed with everything I had that it would happen and never allowed the how to get in the way. In fact, I never made the how my business. I just released the desire to the universe; there was no attachment. This was not the first time or last time I left the how to the universe and simply focused on my what, doing all that I could from where I was.

When Jevon was eight months old, I returned from the USA and gave myself two weeks to find a house to rent in the West Midlands, a three-hour journey from my mother's house in London. I remember telling my plans to my friend Chanel and Jevon's dad, but I could feel their lack of faith. Blah. I did not need their support as universal forces were already at work because I was taking massive action. I booked a coach ticket to the area and stayed with a cousin while I went in search of my apartment. Boom, within a week, I had located an awesome two-bedroomed, ground floor space with an en-suite bathroom, and within two more weeks had signed the lease agreement.

To further illustrate the power of the universe, I also threw into the mix a desire for a car. I wanted it badly because public transportation where I was moving to was ridiculous, and with a young baby and winter fast approaching, walking, catching taxis or the train was difficult. While visiting my cousin and looking for the apartment, I was also searching for cars online, telling others I was on the hunt and working out my finances to enable it to happen. Well, that desire manifested in record time. On the same day I found my apartment, my cousin gave me her old car. Gratitude, excitement, relief and happiness flooded my body as I had manifested two major things I desired in one day. Not once did I worry about the how, just having a strong desire, keeping the faith and taking massive action daily in the direction of my dreams and goals.

Now, to illustrate this point in business, my goal was to hit $5k in sales in one month. I knew how this could be achieved, however I did not know where the clients would come from, so I started doing more from where I was: Facebook, live videos, writing articles, posting on Instagram, connecting with new individuals on social media and through network events, and speaking engagements. From one speaking engagement, I had this phenomenal idea to offer a free coaching intensive through raffle tickets. For the women who did not win, I had a way of reconnecting to offer my services, which I did that very weekend. From a free session, three women moved forward with my coaching services, supporting me to reach my financial goal that month.

> *'You can't know either where or when the universe will enter your affairs – only that it will. So just pitch your pitches, take your baby steps, enjoy the journey and prepare to be astounded.'*

> **~ Mike Dooley ~**

Decide what you want and take massive action in the direction of your goals. It really is that simple. Yet, we make this so damn complicated with our fears, negative emotions and the crazy-ass stories we tell ourselves.

In his book, *Leveraging the Universe: 7 Steps to Engaging Life's Magic*, Mike Dooley explains that the way to engage life's magic is to take action without becoming attached to a particular way you will achieve your goal. You must trust that the more you do, the easier it is for the universe to deliver what you have asked for, which, as I mentioned earlier, takes the pressure off feeling as though you have the weight of the world on your shoulders.

# LET US EXPLORE

Whenever I have a goal, I use the following exercise from *Leveraging the Universe: 7 Steps to Engaging Life's Magic* by Mike Dooley.

**Step One**: Draw a large triangle on a piece of paper and then draw a vertical line cutting the triangle in two (top to bottom – fig 1). Ensure the triangle is large enough to house '…all the action steps necessary for a single dream to come true'.

**Step Two**: At the top of the page write your goal/dream and then, in the bottom left-hand corner, write your name. In the bottom right-hand corner, write 'The Universe' (see fig 1 for example).

**Step Three**: On your side of the triangle, write down everything and anything you can think of doing to move you toward achieving your goal. Get practical here; what action steps will create the results you desire? Mike Dooley says you must write down all you can do spiritually, logically and physically.

**For example, if you desire to start a business, here are some steps you could take:**

- *Find a mentor*
- *Create a business plan*
- *Attend networking events*
- *Start a social media page and post great content*
- *Start a video blog/YouTube channel*
- *Get an accountability partner/create a mastermind group*
- *Read How-To books on your subject/business idea*
- *Carry out market research*
- *Talk to entrepreneurs who are successful in the same field*

**Step Four**: On the side of the triangle labelled 'The Universe', write down all the miracles, coincidences and magic you could experience on your journey toward your goal. This side you will dedicate to everything and anything you could not do by yourself, where you know the universe can have your back.

**Here are some ideas to get you thinking about all that is possible:**

- *You get a gut feeling to go somewhere or do something and you end up meeting someone who can support you toward your goal*
- *Help you to identify possible solutions to your current problem*
- *You are inspired by something you read or heard when you needed it most*
- *Reveal your blocks to success*
- *Arrange circumstances which make it easier for you to move forward*
- *There is so much the universe can do for you; stay open to the magic*

**Step Five**: START TAKING ACTION

*'If you don't do all you can, with what you have from where you are, the Universe cannot do all it can for you.'*

**~ Mike Dooley ~**

**Your Goal Goes Here**

*Figure 1: Goal Triangle*

# CHAPTER 17

# Life Lesson Seventeen

## YOU MUST NOT QUIT IN THE DARK, THE SUN WILL ALWAYS RISE

*'Life is always in motion, so you cannot be "Stuck".'*

**~ Esther Hicks ~**

Starting a business or moving toward success as defined by yourself, requires you to unlearn so much. It will also challenge your childhood beliefs. You must have the tenacity to hold on to faith, when the rest of the world is telling you what you want cannot be done, and you will never make it. That alone causes some individuals to hide and neglect their God-given talent, gifts and power.

**Has there ever been a time when you have felt like quitting?**

I know I am on the right path by using my energy to inspire others, whether that be through writing, speaking, coaching, performing or empowering women through dance. However, since starting in business, there have been multiple excruciating moments when I felt stuck, like giving up and crawling back to my zone of comfort. That is when I would find myself doing the opposite of what I know to work and would sink deeper into a downward-spiralling, drama-filled zone of depression, not knowing when I would be able to lift my head and breathe in hope again.

I have come to realise there will be times in life when the illusions will overpower what we know to be true deep down, and for a moment – which often feels like forever – we sink into the darkness. It is at this point we will most feel like quitting. We may lose hope and question our abilities and judgement; our faith can also be challenged and, in times of real hardship and heartbreak, sometimes we may give up on God. You never know how long you will feel trapped in the dark; it depends on so many factors, but mostly it depends on your willingness to recognise why you are there and your endeavour to find balance, inner peace and happiness again.

My biggest lesson; it is crucial to continue to have hope and faith, trusting you will eventually find your way back to the light. That is, of course, if you want to. Many of us have quit moving toward the very thing we have asked for, just before our miracle occurred, as we did not know along the journey we would face moments so dark.

## Accept Your Present Reality

After three years of 'figuring out' entrepreneurship and hoping for a better day (without consistently putting in the hard work) I had to face my current reality. I was broke and business was far from booming. I had created the reality I found myself in as of February 2018, and I was sick and tired of the fucking struggle. I was in a dark place, ready to get out, yet it was necessary for me to accept where I was and how I got there in the first place. Refusing to pick up a job while I started building my dreams had a lot to do with it. A lack of consistency, urgency and playing small also had something to do with my lack of results. In that moment, I decided I was ready to move toward the light. A better day was coming very soon.

## Find a Reason to Keep Moving Forward

*'We can all get to a very dark place when we cannot see the light, we begin to lose hope. There must be a reason to keep on going.'*

**~ David Neagle ~**

- *What is your why? I asked you this a few Life Lessons ago*
- *Why do you want to be successful?*
- *What does building a brand or business mean to you?*

When you feel stuck, demotivated or trapped, you must focus on what you are moving toward, lean in to your desires and purpose, allowing that to guide you out of the dark. We will all face dark periods, which are necessary to appreciate the better days, so what can you use to keep hope alive when a part of you feels like it is being sucked into a hell which you cannot escape?

Get clear on your reason for doing all you do. Your why. Hold on to the vision you have created. See it in your mind all the time and believe with every fibre in your body you will experience all you envision. This will give you the strength to begin moving through the dead zone of inactivity or fear and back into the light of awareness, vision and good energy.

Do not allow the how to interfere with the vision you keep in the front of your mind. That would make you question your goals. 'Vision' can mean a few things, but you want to create a big-picture vision, and choose aspects of that vision to keep at the forefront of your mind's eye. For example, if you want a grand house, see the kitchen, the bath, the bedroom. Open the front door in your mind and walk into your house; visualise what you want.

If, like me, you want to help people in some way, visualise yourself as a speaker; see the stage, the happy faces of those you have helped, shake their hands. In other words, make this real to your subconscious and the mind will reinforce it for you. If your mind plays tricks with you, bringing up past negative experiences (you tripped going on the stage, forgot your lines, whatever), see yourself laughing at the mistake. In this way, you have reinforced the experience to be more positive than negative.

When you expose your negative thoughts and fears to the light of day, and see them clearly and objectively, you can change your perspective of those events so you can expect more positive experiences. You have made way for them to come in.

## What Is Your Next Best Step?

When we find ourselves in the dark, trying to figure out a masterplan can be a pain in the ass and a detriment to finding your way back to the light. It can be overwhelming. Instead, start with one step and see it through. Each step will naturally lead you to the next. Do not be afraid of being flexible. Your plan is your plan, but along the way you will likely meet obstacles. Do not let that deter you. Just adjust the plan and, eventually, if it is sound and reasonable, it will lead to where you desire to be.

Which brings up another small caveat: Is the plan sound and reasonable? Do not over-extend; your vision will happen on a timeline. Generally, the bigger the vision, the more steps there will be to getting there. If you want that grand house, there will be many steps along the way, but that does not mean you cannot achieve this.

Miracles happen every day, but setting a timeline for the steps you are taking will keep you focused. It will also remind you of how far you have come in your plan. This can be very motivating. The more you do, the closer you get to your goal. The closer you get to your goal, the more you will want to continue the work.

In February 2018, the next best thing I could have done for myself was to get a job, which I did with urgency. One Saturday night I declared that within thirty days or fewer, I would be working. I knew breaking free of the money struggle was what I needed to get back to my purpose so that I could write, coach, teach and speak alongside everything else that was in store for my life. It was not going to happen from that dark place as I did not have the energy, focus or desire to show up consistently. I sent out 100 applications in three days and was offered a job within five, although I held on to the faith that a better offer would present itself, which it did. The pay was more than I had anticipated, and although the hours were longer than I had hoped, I was ready to do what I had to do so that eventually I could do what I desired.

## The Sun Will Always Rise

On the other side of the pain and despair you feel have wrapped you in a thick black cloak, is your breakthrough and lesson. I wholeheartedly believe that 'this too shall pass' applies in any situation, so I try to look for what I can learn from the experience I am going through at any given time. With the one I described above, I learned that:

- *We are never stuck*
- *Miracles can happen quickly if you are open to receiving them*
- *You do not need to know the how, remain focused on the what*
- *I am a powerful chick and manifesting Queen*
- *A better day will always come your way, as it did for me*
- *Struggling was a choice*
- *I can change my reality if I do not like the present one*
- *Focusing on what I wanted as opposed to what I did not want would bring about a change*
- *Commitment is essential for results*

It is learning to see in the darkness and finding our way back to the light that builds our strength, character and faith in what is possible, belief in ourselves, and a belief the universe completely has our back. Hold on to your why if you find yourself feeling stuck and ask, 'What can I do today that will enlighten me and show me a path?' Take the first step. I know you got this.

*'Don't quit. Never give up trying to build the world you can see, even if others can't see it. Listen to your drum and your drum only. It's the one that makes the sweetest sound'*

**~ Simon Sinek ~**

145

# LET US EXPLORE

Too often, we forget the strength, resilience and power we possess. Forgetting this is what can cause us to succumb to the trappings of despair and hopelessness. It all appears too much, and giving up feels like the next best step. The following exercise is designed to help you remember your victories, comebacks and wins, which will support you in times of hardship. When you focus on all you have already accomplished, you reignite that spark of greatness and again have the unwavering faith to crush your biggest goals.

**Think of three accomplishments in your life and answer the following using the table provided**

|  | **One** | **Two** | **Three** |
|---|---|---|---|
| **Describe the accomplishment** |  |  |  |
| **What challenges did you face?** |  |  |  |
| **How did you overcome these challenges?** |  |  |  |
| **Describe the biggest lesson you learned** |  |  |  |
| **How has the experience allowed you to grow as a person?** |  |  |  |

# CHAPTER 18

# Life Lesson Eighteen

## INVEST TO PROGRESS

Investing in yourself to progress can seem daunting, extravagant, scary even; regardless, this is paramount to helping you build a business.

- *Imagine having a front row seat to view some of the most successful individuals sharing their rise to greatness and success secrets with you*
- *Imagine learning the major mistakes of someone who has created massive success doing something you wish to do. Imagine with their support your success is fast-tracked because you are prepared and avoid many of the mistakes, challenges and obstacles they met*
- *Imagine having someone support you from where you are now to where you desire to be, giving you a step-by-step guide and holding you accountable to turn your dreams into reality*

We already have access to the great minds through all the powerful books written throughout the years. There are also courses, online workshops, seminars, live events, audio books and so much more. My question is: are you investing your money and energy in seeking the knowledge that, when applied, will support you to move yourself forward?

Investing in a ticket to a seminar, workshop, event or even a course can open your mind to a new way of living and conducting business, and give you the opportunity to meet like-minded individuals.

Right now, you may be thinking: *this all sounds good, but I do not have the funds to invest in myself right now. Are you ready for my response?*

I call that bullshit!

I am not here to be rude, or tell you what you do or do not have in your bank account, but over the last three years I have personally experienced the power of faith backed by desire and a commitment to a goal or purpose. I have manifested money for my desires and personal development every single time, even at the last minute (sometimes it was a late payment, but the money always came). I wholeheartedly believe the money will show up, but there is a catch. You must be all in and committed to what you say you want. That way the universe knows you are serious and the money will be there for you. My way of thinking has not always been like this, but the last three years have led me to believe God is our supply, and with that being said, 'all things are possible'.

I had a strong desire to become a success coach and help transform other people's lives, although as I previously mentioned, I had this dream-crushing belief one had to become a millionaire before they could speak and write on success. I was no millionaire, so felt I had no voice or authority to support individuals in the way I desired, until I came across Gina DeVee. Her course was a year long, and I knew from the start I wanted in.

Let me explain where I was in this moment. I had never invested in myself at the level of multiple figures, consistently told myself I was broke, was being assisted by the government, and about to move back into my mother's house. I did not feel or see myself as the woman who would or could invest more than $15,000 to move toward my dream. Regardless of where I was at, something inside of me said *get on the phone with them*, my thought process being that the sales associate would help me come up with a way to get on the course. I was already sold; the money was simply not in the bank, or so I thought.

Fast-forward to the phone conversation and, as predicted, the sales associate supported me in exploring ways I could come up with the $2k deposit to get on the course. But, for every path she suggested, I had a reason why that would not work. I even told her I would wait until 2017 to begin because then I would have the money. Truth is, I probably would never have come up with the money; it was fear keeping me from figuring out a way to make what I wanted happen, and a lack of resourcefulness, not resources. Fear of the course not being value for money, fear I would not get results, fear I could not afford the course; I was just plain scared, yet somewhere deep inside I knew this was the change I needed, no matter the price.

## 'I Choose Me'

Something miraculous happens when you get out of your own way long enough to see what is possible from a place of faith instead of fear, where you are looking at what you cannot achieve. The sales associate suggested I take the time to figure out how I would come up with the money, which did not take long. That night I realised I had £1,500 in savings and the rest I could place on a credit card. Can you believe it? I had the money yet I was so caught up in my broke mentality that I missed seeing what was already available.

How often are you doing the same thing?

Investing in a high-level coaching programme changed the game for me, and as a result my learning and development have become non-negotiable. I desire support at every level. I have had coaches for fitness, business and energy healing, and I have an amazing coach helping me (or should I say pushing me) to complete this book in good time. I will keep it real; sometimes I have had to borrow the money from my mother, a family friend, make the money through my business, or put it on a credit card, yet one thing is sure, the money always comes when you are ready and committed to a goal, so do not give up before your demonstration.

## What Should I Be Investing in to Move My Life Forward?

I believe one of the most important investments you can make is to hire a coach/mentor, ensuring your coach also has a coach, mentor, mastermind group or someone to support them to consistently develop. You want to know the person you are investing in is committed to their development and growth as much as you are, or even more, to make sure you receive next-level guidance and support.

If you are thinking of hiring a coach, my advice to you is get ready to:

- *step out of your comfort zone*
- *look at yourself and the action or lack thereof from an objective standpoint*
- *be willing to call yourself out*
- *have your core beliefs challenged*
- *be asked to take massive action beyond what you have ever done*
- *show up consistently to achieve your goals*
- *keep your mind wide open; drop resistance to change*

You have also got to want your results and be willing to do whatever it takes. The coach is not there to carry you on your journey, just to guide you along the way. My advice is to listen to your coach with an open mind. That is what you are paying them for.

## Neither Time Nor Money is Your Real Problem

When it comes to investing in yourself, be honest. Have you used either a lack of time or money as the key reason you could not take the next step? I've done this plenty of times before I became aware of self-sabotage and limiting beliefs. Sometimes we will be afraid to invest because we do not believe in ourselves and our ability to get the results we seek. This is why I often point out the need to constantly check in with self and become awake to the emotions, fears and beliefs we are holding on to. Once you clear this stuff, you can always figure out how you will create the time or come up with the money to do something that will help you to progress. Non-negotiables are simply that. No discussion; it must happen. Once you make investing in your own development non-negotiable, you will open yourself up to a whole new world.

# LET US EXPLORE

Write down a minimum of ONE way you will invest in yourself in the next thirty days, to move toward a goal you have set

_____

_____

Write down any fears, beliefs or stories that will stop you from making this investment

_____

_____

Write down the truth of this situation. What do you know in your heart to be true? What do you know to be exaggerated or built on a false premise?

_____

_____

I do not want money to be the reason you do not take the shot. Below are fifteen ways you can create the money to 'invest in yourself, to progress':

- Savings
- Credit card
- Mother/father
- Spouse
- Bank loan
- Ex
- Friends or family
- Sell your old stuff
- Create a product/ service to sell
- Network marketing
- Business
- Get a job
- Influencer marketing
- Affiliate marketing
- Baby-sitting/Pet sitting

# CHAPTER 19

# Life Lesson Nineteen

## SURROUND YOURSELF WITH POWERFUL PEOPLE

*'You become like the people you spend the most time with.'*

**~ Jim Rohn ~**

This is a simple yet powerful quote, and I bet it is not the first time that you have heard the saying, 'you are the average of the five people you hang around with'. Now is the time to get real with yourself. Who are you spending most of your time with? Are they building you up, calling you out on your shit, encouraging you to chase your dreams, and keeping it 100 with you?

## Confidence is Contagious

Especially when starting a business, you are going to want to connect with people who are on a similar journey, who understand the entrepreneurial path and can support you to take your next steps when the rest of the world is telling you to take a seat. It is suggested you surround yourself with individuals who have already achieved what you want, and do not be afraid to take notes on how they got to that position. I have had the pleasure of connecting with some positive and powerful individuals over the last few years, and it has transformed my life for the better.

The first powerful community I was a part of was the Divine Living Academy 'round 3'. I admit, in the beginning, intimidation was written all over my face. I was around women earning multiple six figures, many who were older and had already reached a high level of success. Also, I was slightly uncomfortable being one of just a few black women in a group of more than 200. However, that feeling passed quickly. I came into the group feeling like I could not be my true self but left empowered, knowing regardless of where we are in our journey and how much money we make, we all have our own issues, wounds and fears to overcome. I was successful in my own right and could also learn a lot from the amazing women I met. But I had to let go of judging and my fear of being judged and allow myself to simply connect in an authentic way.

Megan J Huber is one of my mentors and another powerful person I stay close to. Megan is consistently sharing words of wisdom, strategies for managing your time, teaching others how to develop as a leader, and how to build a six-figure business. When Megan joined the network marketing company, Monat, she invited me to join her on the journey. After overcoming the fear of being a network marketer, I jumped at the chance to be surrounded by and learn from a group of multiple six-figure earners daily for a one-time payment of £350. For me, being in the community was more important than building the marketing business. I have gained more from that business than I ever expected, including lifelong friendships, mastermind partners and the opportunity to create money at will. Being part of a high-vibe entrepreneurial community is a gift as, when plugged in, you feed off the energy of others, push yourself to go further than ever before, learn to take risks, and you have a consistent group of women and men pushing you to be better.

# Find a Community of Powerful People

I have coached many women who felt they had to do life all by themselves, rarely asking for help for fear of becoming a burden to others. In the beginning, I did not have a community and I did not have mastermind partners. The journey was lonely and I was attempting to figure it all out on my own. Do not do what I did. Start now to find your community. You may also want to consider creating your own group of powerful individuals down the line. You may be thinking where do I find my community of successful people? Here are some suggestions for you:

- *Attend networking events*
- *Join (or create) a Meetup group*
- *Volunteer for positions that will put you around other successful individuals*
- *Join a professional association*
- *Attend courses and seminars*
- *Join a network marketing company*
- *Hire a mentor and engage in their community*
- *Talk to more people during your daily activities*

*'Set your life on fire. Seek those who fan your flames.'*

**~ Rumi ~**

# LET US EXPLORE

## You Choose Those Around You

I want to close this Life Lesson by reminding you that you have a choice about who you are around. If the relationships are no longer serving you, if the individuals in question are draining your energy, telling you your dreams are impossible, speaking negatively of others, complaining instead of acting, then it is time to re-evaluate your circle. I am not telling you that you must let go of everyone, however it is important to consider who you are spending a large chunk of your time with and ask yourself, *'are they bringing me down or building me up?'* You have the power to set boundaries, let people know what you will and will not accept, and decrease the amount of time you spend with people who are negatively affecting your life.

When I first started college, I was part of a group of four girls who got lunch together, hung out after college and went shopping during our free periods. A few months into college it was clear these girls were not very serious about their education, as I was. My focus was on leaving with the highest qualification possible, which I achieved. So I began to hang out with them less and less until we pretty much just said hello in passing. Two years later, two out of the three did not pass the course. Imagine if we had continued to rub shoulders daily? Where would I have been after two years of college? You get to choose those around you; it is always a choice, so when you feel obligated to stay around someone you would rather distance yourself from, I want you to create an awareness around the why behind it.

**What do you fear will happen if you no longer associate yourself with this person/group?**

---

---

_____

_____

_____

_____

_____

**How will decreasing your time with this person/group impact your life?**

_____

_____

_____

_____

_____

_____

**What uncomfortable conversation do you need to have to move forward positively?**

_____

_____

_____

_____

_____

_____

_____

**By when will you have this conversation?**

_____

_____

_____

_____

_____

_____

_____

**By decreasing your time spent with these individuals, what do you feel about yourself?**

_____

_____

_____

_____

_____

_____

_____

**What Is the truth of the situation?**

_____

_____

_____

_____

_____

# CHAPTER 20

# Life Lesson Twenty

## TRANSFORM YOUR RELATIONSHIP WITH MONEY

*'...most people never get to even the first stages of accumulating wealth. Too often, they are limited by their own beliefs about money and by the question of whether or not they deserve it.'*

**~ Jack Canfield ~**

OMG, transforming my relationship with money and learning things could be different, realising making money does not have to be so damn hard and that money is always available, were new concepts I resisted at the start of my entrepreneurial journey. As I grew in consciousness, this all started to make much more sense. It was not until three years ago I realised that most things I had heard, learned and believed about money were not true.

Again, this is not about blaming or shaming those who influenced your beliefs around money growing up (although I went through a period of strong resentment toward my mother as I noticed I had adopted so many of her negative beliefs around money, and I hated it).

I also felt responsible for her debt while I was growing up, and vowed to make a success of myself to help her out as an adult. When mum stopped taking an interest in the ways I attempted to make this money, I felt unsupported, adding more fire to the unnecessary fuel. I later realised where you are tomorrow is a product of the choices you make today; I could make new choices to experience something totally different when it came to what I believed and how I felt about money. Blame did not have to be an option.

Gina DeVee was one of the first mentors to drill into my head that my relationship with money could change and, as a result, my whole life could improve. I first had to become aware of the stories that were not true which, as I mentioned earlier, was pretty much everything I knew about money. My core belief was 'making money is hard', and that presented a major problem having just started a business. I also had held on to other negative money beliefs such as:

- *You must watch every penny*
- *There is never enough*
- *Money is to be saved/used to pay bills; I felt wrong spending money on desirable items*
- *Struggle is the only way*
- *Credit cards are bad*
- *Money is scarce and one day we may run out*

Then there were the fears that people would not pay me for coaching, and in the beginning they did not. It felt like I was begging individuals to simply try coaching, even though I knew one conversation with me could change the course of someone's life. I was in a consistently low vibration, feeling alone and emotionally unsupported. I was not valuing myself. I was bathing daily in thoughts and beliefs about not being worthy of receiving money for the work I was doing as that would be easy and, according to my beliefs, making money was not supposed to be simple. I hate to admit it, but I did go through a period of comparing myself to others who had started coaching around the same time and were flying high within six months. Upon digging deeper into what changes they were making, it always went back to personal development;

they were consistently developing their wealth consciousness and transforming their money story.

It got worse before it got better. Struggling to make money in my business, I invested more and more into courses, seminars, workshops and coaches in the hope that whatever was 'wrong with me' could be fixed, so I could start making good money from what I loved doing. I got into debt, ruined my credit, considered filing for bankruptcy, and had serious shame around money. There was nothing wrong with me; I simply had to change certain beliefs I had around money and success, stay on my journey and trust that if I continued to do my inner work, take inspired action, focus on what I wanted with a strong desire to achieve and give my all, I would eventually reap the benefits. It is a lesson only hindsight could have taught me.

*'Inside the energy of abundance, there is no struggle, only flow. If you are struggling, there is something about your thinking or your modus that needs adjustment.'*

**~ Stuart Wilde ~**


## Transforming My Relationship with Money

You will get tired of the same shit and eventually say 'fuck the struggle' and admit your life needs more. You will recognise that, like anybody else, you are worthy of all you desire, and this is the time when transforming your money story becomes a necessity. During our last mastermind weekend with Joanna Turner, I decided struggling and Nofisa no longer worked well together and I was willing to pay the price to change the story and the results that followed for good. Considering twenty-seven years were spent in fear around money, I now appreciate it is a journey to the other side and I still have work to do, but I am diligent and focused on the destination. Below are some of the steps I have taken so far, to begin to create a new relationship with money.

## Learn and Then Apply

I have found great pleasure in learning about *The Science of Getting Rich*. There are so many books which teach the exact formula for beginning to change our mindset around money, thus bringing about a change in our finances. It is simply time to pay attention, trust in the process and do what the authors suggest. I spent too many years reading books and sitting on the knowledge without doing what the author advised; now that I am open to miracles of all sizes, I have begun to not only read but apply what I am learning. To my amazement, slowly but surely, life is feeling more magical each day. Here are some of my book recommendations on money consciousness:

**Get Rich, Lucky Bitch! Release Your Money Blocks and Live a First-Class Life**
By Denise Duffield-Thomas

**The Science of Getting Rich**
By Wallace D. Wattles

**Think and Grow Rich**
By Napoleon Hill

**The Law of Divine Compensation: On Work, Money, and Miracles**
By Marianne Williamson

**The Dynamic Laws of Prosperity**
By Catherine Ponder

**The Trick To Money Is Having Some!**
By Stuart Wilde

## Upgrade Me

I once took a six-week money boot camp course hosted by Denise Duffield-Thomas, and one of the most important things she suggests is to upgrade your life. For example, I got rid of all the clothes that made me feel poor and invested in better-quality items that made me feel so good. I also upgraded my make-up and the type of accommodation I stayed in when travelling. I would also go to the hotel lobby to work on my business as the atmosphere was so much more peaceful, attractive and free of clutter than the home I was living in. Starting slowly but surely is the way forward. I have learned that this concept helps us to break the perception of ourselves more than anything. I no longer classed myself as the struggling single mum or the type of person that 'cannot afford' the things she desired. If I want something, it goes on to my upgrade list, which helps me to walk taller, feel more confident and know that life is changing for the better, because I am changing.

## New vs Old Beliefs

A belief is simply a thought one thinks repeatedly. So what would happen if you decided to choose a more positive money belief over the old, negative belief that no longer serves you? I have tried this and, although it can be a challenge, replacing my negative beliefs with positive ones allows me to experience money in a different and more pleasurable way. I also learned the key to moving forward is finding evidence to support that new belief. The more evidence you can find, the stronger the belief. That works for both positive and negative beliefs, and you get to choose where your focus goes.

| Money is scarce | **VS** | There is always enough |
|---|---|---|
| I have no money | **VS** | God is my supply |
| Making money is hard | **VS** | Making money can be easy |
| I cannot afford it | **VS** | What can I do to afford this? |
| Someday I will be rich | **VS** | I am abundant |

To conclude, transforming my money story has been the most challenging experience since beginning in business, as it has taken me so far out of my comfort zone, and again this is only the beginning of the journey. I encourage anyone sitting in fear around money to take the first step; get aware of your current thoughts about and relationship with money and begin doing whatever is required to improve your finances.

You will likely meet with sabotage, fear and resistance along the way. Read, learn, apply, ask for support, and begin to enjoy the fruits of your labour. It is from this place that we are so much more equipped to support others to live out loud.

*'Sorting out your money dramas and daring to live a richer life will give other women permission to do the same... And together we are going to change the world.'*

**~ Denise Duffield-Thomas ~**

# LET US EXPLORE

## Identifying Your Own Money Story

To transform your relationship with money, it helps to know where your beliefs stem from. Answer the following questions honestly, as all the change we experience first begins with awareness of where we are. This is not about making family, friends, guardians, or yourself wrong, it is about identifying where you are so you can move to where you desire to be.

**Growing up, what did you learn about money from your mother/guardian?**

_____

_____

_____

_____

_____

**Growing up, what did you learn about money from your father/guardian?**

_____

_____

_____

_____

_____

_____

_____

**Growing up, what did you see/learn about money from your grandparents?**

_____

_____

_____

_____

_____

_____

**If money were a person, how would you feel toward that individual?**
_(Be honest. How would you treat that person?)_

_____

_____

_____

_____

_____

_____

**What do you feel are the key stories and beliefs you are holding on to, which contribute to your financial circumstances?**

_____

_____

_____

_____

_____

_____

_____

_____

**What is your core belief around money, which could be holding you back from the success you seek?** *(Mine was that life had to be a struggle and making money was hard)*

_____

_____

_____

_____

_____

_____

**What meaning do you give to money?** *(freedom, scarcity, lack)*

_____

_____

_____

_____

_____

_____

_____

Can you recall a really good experience you have had with money? How did that change your feelings toward it?

_____

_____

_____

_____

_____

_____

_____

_____


Can you recall a really bad experience you have had with money? How did that change your feelings toward it?

_____

_____

_____

_____

_____

_____

_____

_____


Now you have an awareness of your current thoughts, feelings, stories and beliefs around money, it is time to do the work. I advise you to begin by reading *The Science of Getting Rich* by Wallace D. Wattles

# CHAPTER 21

# Life Lesson Twenty-One

## YOU CAN MANIFEST MONEY NOW

*'Faith is the evidence of things not seen. You can create things to come into your life that are not yet seen as long as you have the faith they will occur.'*

**~ Gina DeVee ~**

After joining Gina DeVee's transformational coaching course in 2016, my response to my desires began to shift. I started saying yes to the things I wanted to be, do and have even when I had absolutely no freaking clue where I would get the money from. I admit there were times when I doubted myself, let go of my unwavering faith and, of course, the money did not show up for me. How could it? After all, I was all over the place, overwhelmed, wishing, hoping and questioning if a miracle would occur. Yet the times when I held on to the belief that the money would show up, took inspired action and ignored everyone else's unsolicited advice, despite initial appearances, the money always came.

## You Must Commit First

As I mentioned, when signing up for Gina's course, I had no idea how the first instalment was going to get paid. I had used my savings on the deposit for the course, had just qualified as a personal trainer, moved back to London, and began working at Gymbox. Broke and yet to attract my first client, I was living on a prayer. The first instalment was due the end of January, but the money had yet to show up. Although I was based in the gym, I was uncomfortable speaking to the members. Sales did not come easy to me, and fear kept me hidden in the changing rooms most days. Yes, it was a sad sight.

As the countdown to my next payment began, the pressure was on. Although afraid of the idea of rejection, I began to put in the groundwork in the gym by offering free sessions and telling members about the services I offered. About a week to ten days before the payment was due, the gym manager introduced me to a young woman named Jen from New York, who was ready to get in shape for the New Year. We hit it off immediately, and she loved the complimentary training session I offered. Twelve sessions were going to cost her £600, which was the amount I needed for my first payment. Well damn, she paid three days before I needed to make the next instalment. My money miracle occurred.

I have learned we must first commit to doing the things we truly desire before the money shows up. This is the reason, I believe, why many struggle to manifest their desires. Waiting for the money, conditions to be better or the right moment before taking the risk or saying yes to what you want does not work. Believe me, I have tried.

Commitment always comes first. *Why?* I wholeheartedly believe the universe wants us to have all we desire and will support us in every way to get it, but we need to make the first move. Committing to what you want shows how serious you are and, from there, you can begin to unleash life's magic. If you can conceive an idea, it can be achieved. The question is, will you be ready when it arrives? Commitment and action indicate you will be much more prepared.

## The Money Manifesting Formula I Follow

A simple formula extracted from *Get Rich, Lucky Bitch! Release Your Money Blocks and Live a First-Class Life* by Denise Duffield-Thomas is what I use to manifest my desires, and it really works. According to Denise, the formula can be used to manifest whatever it is you desire, if you believe with all your energy what you want is possible. I mostly use this formula to manifest the money to travel or buy something I really want. For example, I used it to manifest a trip to Puerto Rico, and took Jevon and my mother to celebrate her 60th birthday. I highly encourage you to read *Get Rich, Lucky Bitch!* and practise turning your desires into reality. It is a lot of fun seeing what is possible for yourself when you believe, commit and act.

I have provided an outline of the five-step process below, using the example of manifesting my trip to L.A. to attend Marianne Williamson's Miracle Minded New Year's Eve event in 2017. Being present was my miracle, so have fun using the formula and remember it takes practise. If you have not manifested what you want by step five, go back to step one and repeat.

## Declutter Everything in Your Life

*'Don't underestimate the life-changing effects of physically decluttering your life.'*

**~ Denise Duffield-Thomas ~**

One of my most favourite activities is 'The Declutter'. 'Out with the old and in with the new' the saying goes, and this is the first step you must take when going after your goals. Let go of what no longer serves you or brings you joy. Like seriously, do you need that old toaster, jacket, pair of shoes with a hole you have not worn in forever? Let it all go is my motto, and I declutter on average every six to eight weeks. However, when I desire to manifest something specific, I intentionally clear out to make space (energetically) for the new things I am asking for. This step feels amazing, and you will feel lighter, freer and ready to manifest.

I had yet to manifest the money for a plane ticket and accommodation for the event in L.A., so the first thing I did was clear out my room. What old papers, clothes, shoes and books did I no longer need? It was also coming up to a new year, which was another great reason to declutter. I then took the stuff to the charity shop but, if you can, sell it or give your items to someone you know.

## Decide Exactly What You Want

I had to decide (although the money had yet to show up) to be at the Marianne Williamson event in L.A. I had to act like I would be there regardless of appearances, so I scheduled it in my calendar and asked my mother to have my son for the duration of the trip.

## Surround Your Life With Positivity

'Believe before you receive' is a motto I like to use. At times, our faith and hope can dwindle due to appearances, but we cannot powerfully manifest from a place of fear and doubt. Surrounding yourself with positive books, podcasts, people and other resources will help keep your faith strong through this process. I kept Florence Scovel Shinn's book, *The Game Of Life And How To Play It* at hand while going through the process, which helped loads as I was able to keep the faith by reading all the money miracles she had described.

## Take Inspired Action

How was the money going to come to me? My coaching clients were all finishing their programmes, and I was finding it a challenge to attract new clients. However this is not a time to focus on the 'how'. You just need to remain focused on the 'what' and act. What action are you being led to take? Listen for the nudges, look for the signs and act on them immediately. I was led to connect with a lady who was interested in coaching who had yet to commit to a ninety-day package. I was also led to connect with a current client to see if she desired to continue with the work she was doing with me. Pay attention, the universe has your back.

## Receive and Fine-Tune

I spoke with the lady who was interested in my coaching programme. She did sign up and I was able to book my flight to the USA. I paid for the accommodation with money I received from another client. I was in my element. The money showed up for what I desired. With hindsight, I would consider everything I had to pay for or would want to do during my trip and focus on the specific amount of money I desired to manifest, as although I received what I had asked for, I did not manifest enough cash to shop, eat out and enjoy L.A. like I wanted. I did not ask the bank of endless supply for enough and instead focused on the minimum I needed to make it happen. Do not do that; ask for what you really want and take massive action to achieve it.

# LET US EXPLORE

Ready to manifest? You can also use the Triangle Goal Exercise at the end of Chapter Sixteen to help you stay focused.

What do you desire to manifest?

_____

_____

_____

_____

_____

_____

_____

By when would you like to achieve this goal?

_____

_____

Follow the formula and record your experience below.

- _Declutter everything in your life_

_____

_____

_____

_____

_____

_____

- *Decide exactly what you want*

_____
_____
_____
_____
_____
_____
_____

- *Surround your life with positivity*

_____
_____
_____
_____
_____
_____
_____

- *Take inspired action*

_____
_____
_____
_____
_____
_____

- *Receive and fine-tune*

_____

_____

_____

_____

_____

_____

_____

_____

_____

**Date I achieved my goal:**

_____

_____

**My experience using the manifesting formula was...** *(complete the sentence)*

_____

_____

**Next time I will...** *(complete the sentence)*

_____

_____

# PART FOUR

# Life Lessons
# on Motherhood

*'Don't compare yourself to other mothers. We are all losing our shit.*
*Some just hide it better than others.'*

**~ Unknown ~**

## Mothers...

Each one of us has our own story, yet we face the same task, to raise a child. Whether we are the biological parent, grandparent, aunt or guardian, not one of us were given a manual to parenting. We therefore strive to do the best we know how with the tools we currently have. It is messy; we shout, we get frustrated, children will cry, parents cry, screams will be heard. Fun times are plenty, hard times occur. We have proud mama moments and moments when we wish the ground would swallow us up. There will be yeses and many NOs, there are busy days and lazy ones, too; some mothers have guilt, others welcome a break, and at some point we have probably questioned if we are doing this thing called parenthood right. Regardless, our goal is to love, guide and protect our children. However, I am sure you know, whether from experience or watching someone close to you raise children, that this is not always an easy task.

179

A few years after giving birth, I became focused on diving deep into personal development. One thing I have become acutely aware of is the direct impact a mother/guardian's thoughts, communication (or lack of it), feelings, behaviour, secrets, walls, experiences, wounds and beliefs have upon their children, and how this all comes together to shape the child's beliefs and reality. Some will hate to admit it, others have no idea they played a part in creating it, some can see the dysfunction but are unaware of how to end it, and there are others who decide enough is enough and have begun their journey from victim to victor, a powerful experience for all involved.

For the first four years of my child's life, I held on to emotions such as regret, rejection and resentment. I loved my child dearly, however I felt stuck and struggled as a single parent. In my experience growing up, being a single mother meant hardship and struggle and that is the role I took on when I had Jevon. It took coaching, energy healing and transforming my beliefs to create a new story about what was possible for me as a single parent, but the main thing is that I was able to work through the emotions and redesign my life as I wished it to be.

I cannot stress enough the importance of becoming aware of and recognising that the challenges we face and the wounds yet to be healed have a direct impact upon our children and how they grow up. As I continue to do my inner work, breaking the patterns of my family lineage, my wish for so many is to wake up to what is not working for you and discontinue making the same choices and repeating the negative patterns of your parents and their parents. Easier said than done, but awareness is the first step to change, so starting there will be paramount to creating a new reality for yourself and your children.

As I take you through my life lessons from motherhood, I invite you to think about where you are on your journey. If you are considering having children soon, how can you use this period of your life to prepare? Already given birth? Every one of our journeys will be different, yet we can learn so much from someone else's story, lessons and breakthroughs. No children? Whether you have chosen not to have children or for health reasons, you cannot give birth, I invite you to read the next Life Lesson, **You Matter Too** especially. Parent or not, many have forgotten to take care of number one – themselves.

# CHAPTER 22

# Life Lesson Twenty-Two

## YOU MATTER TOO

*'I either have it together, hair, make-up and gorgeous clothes or look a hot mess who dragged herself out of bed that morning. There is no in-between.'*

**~ Welcome to Motherhood ~**

I first want to take a moment to simply celebrate you! Mother or not, I am sure you spend a lot more time taking care of others than you do ensuring your cup is filled up. I learned from Iyanla Vanzant that this is not the best way to do life. Instead one should make sure that first your cup is full; the overflow is what we give to the world because, just like a fountain, if you are constantly being filled up, there will always be an overflow and you will always have enough love, energy, time and focus for others. Take care of you first. It is not selfish. 'It is self-full,' explained Iyanla on a segment with Oprah Winfrey.

This Life Lesson may piss a few off, as it goes against a core belief I know many people hold. That is, once you become a parent, it is 'all about the children', and you become low-priority. This is not a joke. I have heard friends and other women who have coached with me speak these very words. Also, I witnessed my mother raise two children in the same way. Now honey, if this belief is working for you, I give you full permission to skip this section. But I have

183

a strong feeling reading this Life Lesson may serve as a reminder that your happiness, desires, well-being, health and fitness are just as important as the little or big people who look to you as their guardian.

At the time I was pregnant one of my closest friends followed suit, giving birth to a beautiful baby boy just five months after Jevon was born. I was adamant that, as a mother, it was important to still have time to travel, take care of myself, exercise, personally develop and do what I loved. Simone, however, felt differently and she made it clear. One specific conversation still stands out today. We were in her car driving through Brixton and she was suggesting to me that, *'It is not about you any more, Nofisa. Once you are a mother it is all about the child.'* My thought process: this girl is crazy. And I have a strong feeling she believed I was selfish. I wholeheartedly agree if she did think that, as I encourage a healthy dose of selfishness as a parent, because we cannot give what we do not have. How many parents/guardians do you know who are:

- *Exhausted*
- *Angry as soon as they wake*
- *Always complaining*
- *Severely unfit*
- *Pleasure-starved*
- *Lacking confidence*
- *Not making time for themselves*
- *Short-tempered*
- *Slovenly*

If you see yourself in the above description, understand this chapter was not designed to make you feel bad, but to set you free from the belief you are not important, and everyone else's happiness must be put above your own. Think about it; our children are learning from us, so what example are we setting by showing them 'I am not that important'? It can become learned behaviour for our children, having them grow up to believe it is okay to put everyone before themselves, potentially leading to pain, anger and resentment in adulthood. So, let us lead by example and remember, a belief is simply a thought we think repeatedly. That means, at any time, you can choose to begin thinking, 'I am important too', 'my desires matter', 'being a great parent means loving me as much as I love my children'. It may sound weird in the beginning, you may even think this is pointless, but in the long run, giving to yourself and your children will do wonders for all involved.

By the time Jevon was one, my friendship with Simone was coming to the end of that season. I continued to make myself a priority while she began to withdraw to the point we no longer spoke to each other. I guess her adjustment to motherhood was far more challenging than my experience.

I had not seen or heard from Simone in almost five years, until one day she asked a mutual friend if he could give me her number. It was miraculous reconnecting with Simone, as she appeared to be a changed woman. Her fire was back, she was exercising, adored her body and was making plenty of time to enjoy womanhood, no excuses. My advice: do not allow five years to pass by; you can begin to make yourself a priority today. Here are a few ways to ensure YOU time consistently gets into your calendar.

## Pleasure Pledge

I absolutely love Regena Thomashauer. In her book, *Mama Gena's School of Womanly Arts*, she suggests scheduling one pleasurable thing for yourself each week, which I ensure that I do. Whether it is a movie, setting time aside to read, a massage, getting your nails done, or a walk in the park, think about what lights you up and ensure you do a minimum of ONE of these things every week. Tell a friend, spouse or family member what you plan to do so they can hold you accountable and call you out if you fail to dedicate some time to you.

So, what will it be this coming week?

## Lean on Others and Allow Them to Lean on You

'I don't like asking people for favours.' Sound familiar? I used to think that way, but soon realised it was not helping me as a single mother of one with unfulfilled dreams. I learned when I had Jevon that bringing up a child in a loving environment, achieving my goals and keeping my sanity would only be possible if I recruited others to support me. When Jevon joined a nursery in London, he became friends with a little girl his age called Imarni. They have gone on to be in the same class at school and her mother, Sabina, and I became good friends. Leaning on each other has been a gift, as it has allowed us to have time away from our children to focus on the things we desire to do or need to get done. As I write this, Jevon and Imarni are together playing and arguing in my living room and I am awaiting Sabina to collect the two of them so I can focus on writing this book for the remainder of the day. Support each other. That creates a win-win situation.

## Wake Up Before the Kids

We all have the same twenty-four hours in a day; how we use them will determine our quality of life. When I was working full-time, I did not have many people around to look after Jevon and did not feel like paying for childcare to simply go to the gym. Instead, I would put on Shaun T's Insanity Max:30 workout or T25 and get my sweat on before I heard the noises of an alert and hungry toddler. That worked for me, and it could also work for you. My advice to anyone who says they have no time for themselves now they have kids is to change your language and change the story. Ask, 'How can I find the time to...?' It is a game-changer and your sanity depends on a mindset shift.

# LET US EXPLORE

**Over the next thirty days, what pleasurable things will you commit to?**

- *Week One*

_____

_____

_____

_____

- *Week Two*

_____

_____

_____

_____

- *Week Three*

_____

_____

_____

_____

- *Week Four*

_____

_____

_____

_____

**Plan a guilt-free weekend for yourself in the next sixty days and have a bloody great time. Ready? Steady? Plan...** *(Don't have children... Well, what are you waiting for?)*

- *Date*

_____

- *Who will the children stay with?*

_____
_____
_____
_____
_____
_____

- *What activities will you do?*

_____
_____
_____
_____
_____
_____
_____

**First things first: book childcare and activities so you are committed to making this happen. No excuses; you matter too.**

# CHAPTER 23

# Life Lesson Twenty-Three

## PREPARE FOR THEIR FUTURE

### Pay Your Child First

When Jevon was born I set up an individual savings account (ISA) in his name, which cannot be touched before his eighteenth birthday. It is unfortunate that I viewed money very differently in the early years of his life and, thinking I could not afford to save, I failed to commit to putting even a small amount of money aside on a regular basis. However, beginning later is better than never getting started at all so, around age four, I decided to set up a standing order which ensures money is deposited from my bank account to his weekly. I took this concept from a chapter in *The Success Principles* by Jack Canfield: 'Pay yourself first.' I am both amazed and excited at how quickly his money is growing. In short, instead of paying for everything and then trying to save from what is left, I ensure the money is deducted first, so there are no excuses. Then I focus on doing what must be done and enjoying leisure activities with the money left over.

### Love Insurance (Have You Got Yours?)

One of my mentors often says, 'If I die tomorrow, I want to ensure that today I am living large'. Well, words to that effect. It sounds morbid, but it helps her to fully show up every day and be the woman she was called to become. Taking out a life insurance policy to support your children and family in the event of your death may sound morbid and like something you do not want to think about, but we cannot control the future. We can find peace in knowing if anything was to happen to us, the people we care about would be supported financially.

*'It's hardly surprising that most of us try to avoid thinking about death. However, a failure to consider and discuss the consequences should the worst happen can leave those we love in serious financial difficulty.'*

### ~ Jody Baker ~
*CompareTheMarket.com*

My aunt had been nagging me about taking out a life insurance policy for years and I see now the importance of doing so. Desreen Brooks, aged thirty-three, a wife and mother to two-year-old Jackson, took out life insurance a mere eight months before she was killed in a car incident. Initially, Desreen and her husband, like so many individuals (including myself at one point), did not see the need for life insurance. They were young with what they thought were their whole lives ahead of them. Yet one evening she was swiftly taken from her family right before their eyes. Fortunately, the insurance policy supported her husband and son to buy a new home and pay for the emotional support needed to deal with Desreen's death.

Research conducted in the UK in 2016 suggests failure to take out life insurance puts approximately 3.6 million families at financial risk if adversity strikes. Insurance can cost less than £10 per month depending on your age and other factors affecting the premium such as health.

Do not bury your head in the sand; begin to prepare for your children's future, starting today by saving money regularly and taking out a life insurance policy to protect them in the event you are not here to do so.

# LET US EXPLORE

**I have a savings account for my children**   Y ☐   N ☐

- *(If no) The date I will open a savings account for my child(ren) is*
  _____

- *The amount of money I will commit to saving is* _____
  *per week/month*

**I have a life insurance policy**   Y ☐   N ☐

- *If no, what are your fears/concerns/resistance around taking out an insurance policy?*

_____

_____

- *What are the benefits to having a policy in place?*

_____

_____

**If you have yet to take out an insurance policy, are you ready to do so now?**   Y ☐   N ☐

- *If yes, by what date will you do so?*

*Date:* _____

- *If no, what are your reservations?*

*Reservations:* _____

# CHAPTER 24

# Life Lesson Twenty-Four

## YOUR BODY IS POWERFUL

*'85% of the moms who were overweight one to two years later blamed pregnancy for their weight problem.'*

**Babycentre.com**
*'The New-Mom Body Survey: 7,000 Women Tell It How It Is'*

I was returning to the UK recently and, as I sat in the airport lounge waiting to board the flight, I overheard a woman talking about her body, so I leaned in and listened. 'I tell my daughter all the time, you made mommy fat,' she laughed, yet it was clear this was not actually a joke to her. I admit, the way she shared her story made me laugh. Regardless, I believe both you and I can absolutely work toward achieving the body we want even now that we have children. Notice I said '...the body we want', as too often we get caught up trying to please others, so no more blaming, or complaining. I have learned that it is possible to transform your body. The question is how bad do you want results?

At this point you may be thinking, *well Nofisa, easy for you to say because you do not have a mummy tummy to lose,* to which I would respond, I too had a mummy tummy and it is my mindset and habits, in addition to my belief in what was possible, which have been the driver of all that I have achieved with my body post-pregnancy.

However, I have had plenty of ups and downs with my weight over the last six years also, depending on where my head was at in any given season. For the woman who has given up on ever living with a body she loves, who has struggled to feel comfortable in her skin after having a baby and is ready for change, I created this chapter in the hope the steps I took to achieve a body I loved post-pregnancy will support you to begin or continue your journey.

## Losing the Mummy Tummy

I will admit, I was super-conscious about having a mummy tummy post-pregnancy, so immediately began preparing my body to make it easier to bounce back after giving birth. I enlisted the help of Julie Tupler. Really what that means is I invested about £20 in her two books, *Maternal Fitness* and *Lose Your Mummy Tummy*, and began to do the suggested exercises consistently. It really worked. Although my tummy was expanding, my core muscles were still being trained, so when it came time to have Jevon (I had a C-section), the doctors struggled to get to him as my muscles were strong and difficult to separate. I vividly remember laying on the table, watching them pull very hard to separate my abs. The doctor told me I had one of the strongest core muscles they had seen, and I owe a lot to Ms Tupler and her techniques, demonstrated in the above books.

It is not too late to work on your tummy. The book also invites women who do not have kids to do these exercises, so I recommend checking out The Tupler technique as soon as possible. Just remember, you have to do the work. Another friend was also having a baby just after me and I gave her the book once I gave birth, yet she never got the desired results. It was not that she did not know how or have the tools to get started, she simply never decided to lose her mummy tummy. That does not have to be your reality. Decide and commit today to get started on your best-body-ever journey, taking it at your own pace but making consistent progress toward your goal.

## What Are You Capable Of?

In 2015, I signed up for a female fitness modelling competition. Until then I did not realise I could ever have visible abs or take my body to the next level in the way I did. The most powerful gift I received from entering the competition was the ability to see what I was capable of.

I had lost all my baby weight and more rather quickly after having Jevon. Regardless, by the time he was two years old I did not have a consistent workout routine or way of eating, and I began to see the weight creep back on. It was not until I met Kelly (a fitness model who was now supporting women to compete) at a Body Power convention in Birmingham that I began to believe if others could start from a similar weight and shape as me and achieve great results then, hell, I could too. I now had a vision of my best body ever and, to hold me accountable, I signed up to compete in the Miss Galaxy Universe fitness model competition a mere five months later. I had one major goal in mind; to win the Yummy Mummy category in the hope of inspiring other mamas to take the necessary steps to achieve the results they desired. I was nervous, excited, scared and ready for change, so I signed up to Kelly's body transformation program within two weeks of meeting her and began my journey.

Showtime came around faster than ever, and although Kelly and her coaching skills did not carry me to the finish line, as she predicted, my body was banging. Looking back at where I was when I started in May to where I finished in November was shocking for me in a good way, yet other family members had plenty to say.

- *You are too skinny*
- *You are too muscular*
- *You have lost all your curves*
- *I am not keen on your new look*

That was all cool with me, as I was not changing my body to please anyone but myself and empower others to do the same in the

195

process. People will always have something to say, but you must live for what lights you up. It is funny, those very same family members were the first to notify me when I put on weight after the show. I digress. Let us now get back to my main point. I attribute my success to the power of a goal, knowing the why, being supported and never quitting. Now, let me break these areas down further, as following these exact steps continues to work for me today.

## The Power of a Goal

*'Whatever goal you give to your subconscious mind, it will work night and day to achieve.'*

**~ Jack Canfield ~**

I had a goal of being stage-ready and taking home a medal at the Miss Galaxy Universe competition on November 7th, 2015. My goal was measurable, as anyone could ask me on the evening of the 7th, 'Did you take home a medal?' I either met my goal or I did not. Jack Canfield expresses the need to have specific goals you can measure to unleash the power of your subconscious mind. For example, you may want to get in the best shape to run a marathon or lose ten pounds by your next birthday. Whatever you desire, stop saying you simply want to lose weight or get fit. Get super-specific, then add a deadline to help motivate you to begin or else it ends up being a wish or just another thing that would be nice to do.

## Get Support

There is great power in being held accountable to do what you said you would do long after you said it. When you no longer feel like putting in the work, having support will help motivate, get you back on track, allow you to see ups and downs are expected along the journey and celebrate your wins with you. Be warned; NOBODY can want the results for you more than you do yourself, so if no effort or a lack of commitment is evident on your part, do not expect to have your mentor, fitness trainer or coach stay committed to your goals either.

Unsure where to find support? Ask around, put up a social media post for recommendations, look at others getting results and ask how they did it. There is so much support for us, we just need to get out of our own way long enough to take consistent action and win.

## Know Your Why and Never Quit

Along your health and fitness journey, there will be times when you want to throw in the towel for sure. In the months leading up to my competition especially, I became demotivated, struggled to stay on the diet plan and thought about quitting more than once. But then how could I sit here writing this paragraph for you today? I had to commit until the end. For the mama reading this, you are one of my biggest whys. I want to live my best life, feel amazing in my body, show other mamas what is possible, and support you to do the same in your life. I had to keep going, and once you know your why and allow it to be stronger than your fears and obstacles, although there will be times when quitting seems the best option, you will keep going and achieve your goals.

I believe in you...

*P.S. I walked away from the Miss Galaxy Universe competition with three medals: First place in Yummy Mummy; second place for Fitness Model; first place for my pole dance routine in the category Showgirl. One thing is for sure, I did not come to play.*

**I believed I was a Hott Mama, and so it was**

## LET US EXPLORE

**Describe your ideal body** *(How do you feel? What is your body capable of?)*

_____

_____

_____

_____

**What is the first step you can take to move toward the vision above?**

_____

_____

**What new habits will you need to adopt to achieve your desired goal?**

_____

_____

**Pick the habit that will make the biggest difference for you now and focus on this habit consistently over the next ninety days** *(Record your changes, breakthroughs, wins below)*

_____

_____

_____

_____

_____

_____

# CHAPTER 25

# Life Lesson Twenty-Five

## IT IS NOT ABOUT YOU: CO-PARENTING AFTER THE BREAK-UP

You may be thinking, *girl didn't you just say it is not all about the kids and I matter too three chapters ago? Now suddenly it is not about me?* Confused? Don't be. Let me explain. Just because a relationship ends, it does not mean a war has to begin. As a mother, I believe you should balance taking care of your children with ensuring you are taking care of yourself, also. It is necessary. But, when there is a break-up, I believe it is important for parents to not make it about them and their pain and instead think about how they can best parent together moving forward, if that is an option. I am not in any way, shape or form suggesting that you do not deal with your hurt, anger, feelings of rejection or other painful emotions, but using your child to punish the other parent should not be the outlet for those feelings. Yet how many families do you know who are going through a situation like this?

### You Are Responsible for Your Pain, Even If it is Someone Else's Fault

I was talking to a guy I was interested in recently and he was sharing a personal story about how the mother of his eight-year-old daughter behaves toward him, and I was shocked. He told me the mother has already made it clear that if he gets into a relationship with another woman, she plans to create hell for them both (by the way it did not work out for us, so I escaped that drama). I know there is a lot more to that story than he ever let on, but this is an all-too-common issue among parents today. I write this chapter as an invitation for anyone feeling they cannot let go of someone who no longer wants to be with them, or feels the need to punish your child's other parent because you have yet to forgive them for the hurt that passed between the two of you.

It is important to seek support to move through this period, because you are not only hurting yourself with this behaviour – your children suffer the most. Remember, you had a life before the relationship and you can have an amazing life after, too, but first accept the other parent has moved on and it is your responsibility to heal the wounds you have. It is not their responsibility, no matter how badly you feel they have hurt you. Nobody can do the inner work for you.

## It Does Not Have to Be Like the Movies

In movies, we often see bickering, fights and hate between broken families, and I have, more than once, had to remind Jevon's father I am the mother of his child. I do not disrespect him and I ask that he treat me in the same way. 'Get out of your feelings and show up as the parent,' I have caught myself saying when I have felt he has handled things from a place of being difficult and not in Jevon's best interest.

Jevon was staying with his dad for Christmas and I insisted he take me to where my son would be during that time. He said I was like the FBI needing to know everything, however when Jevon was a few months old, in jest he threatened to take Jevon back to Haiti and joked there was nothing I could do if that happened. So I simply covered my back and made sure I knew where he lived before leaving our child for the week. When I was leaving, Jevon and his dad accompanied me to the car park, and as I moved toward the door, a lady held it open for me, then walked through toward the flats without a word. I caught on to the fact this was his partner as he tried to stop her, but his attempts were futile and she sashayed past us. I later cursed him for not introducing us and encouraged him to do so the next time. It simply was not good enough. I do not want to raise my son in a hostile environment, so being able to be civil with both my son's father and his partner is important to me. On the next encounter, his partner got out of the car and hugged me. *What a transformation*, I thought.

Our adult problems do not have to become our children's issues. It is important we take time to learn the skills to deal with our emotions so we stop repeating family patterns and instead allow our children to see what a healthy parenting relationship can look like. When you show up differently, you will be surprised to see the other parent may also change the way they respond to you. I encourage you to allow your children to form their own opinions of the other parent through their own observations; how they show up for those children, how they treat you now and how they behave in general. Again, do not allow your personal feelings toward your ex influence how you present them to your child (such as in name calling).

# LET US EXPLORE

*'The key to successful co-parenting is to separate the personal relationship with your ex from the co-parenting relationship.'*

**www.helpguide.org**

**Communication is key in any relationship, and improving how you connect with your ex can have many benefits**

**Describe your level of communication with your ex**

_____

_____

_____

_____

_____

_____

_____

_____

**How do you feel about your relationship now you are separated?**

_____

_____

_____

_____

_____

_____

_____

How can you improve the communication to ensure your children experience the best of both parents growing up?

_____

_____

_____

_____

_____

_____

_____

_____

_____

_____

_____

_____

Do you feel you have forgiven your ex for all that has passed between the two of you?

_____

_____

_____

_____

_____

_____

_____

_____

_____

_____

_____

_____

**If no, what can you commit to moving forward to forgive, heal and be a better parent for your children?** *(writing a forgiveness letter, coaching, counselling, energy healing)*

_____

_____

_____

_____

_____

_____

_____

_____

_____

_____

_____

_____

_____

_____

_____

_____

# Life Lesson Twenty-Six

## CHILDREN ARE A BLESSING

*The news you were coming took me by surprise*
*Emotions suddenly filled my soul, whilst tears welled in my eyes*
*It wasn't because I was happy, neither was I sad*
*Simply put, it was unexpected; I feared the world would*
*see me as bad*
*Yet quickly, all those feelings drifted away*
*As I knew you were a blessing, here to stay*

**~ A Note to My Unborn Child ~**

## Jevon: 'Gift of God'

IN DENIAL! No other phrase could describe me better in that moment. I suspected there was a baby growing inside me, but I did nothing and told nobody. Lethargy, a missed period, the most painful boobs, and my passion for pole had diminished, yet I continued to ignore the signs. Intuition told me what was to come, however if there was no proof, I did not have to face my truth. Ever felt like that? Refusing to face the truth so that you do not have to deal with it?

The longer you play ignorant, the less discomfort you experience, but that is not real. By ignoring our truths, we fail to deal with things as they are and instead see things as we wish them to be, with rose-coloured glasses on. Falling asleep on the job became routine, people began to suspect what was growing within, but nobody spoke a word and I was reluctant to confide in anyone about how I felt. The fear of a pregnancy test coming back positive kept me in limbo for a few weeks. I was not ready to be a mama, I did not want my life to change and, I admit, fear of what people would think plagued my mind at night, when the rest of the city slept.

The universe must have gotten tired of my B.S. and refusal to deal with the situation, and gave me a big fat sign to take the next step. Let us face it, there is only so long you can hide from the truth with a large-headed baby growing inside you. My time was up and I would soon learn my fate. Driving with my son's father early one morning, we stopped at traffic lights and something told me to look up. Right before my eyes was a massive building, housing the largest sign which read: *Think You Are Pregnant? Call number now to schedule your free pregnancy test.* Well damn. Talk about perfect timing. It is laughable now, because the universe could not have been more direct, and I could not go on alone in this process. Help was recruited, and Lord knows I was going to need it.

## Your Blessings Often Come Disguised as Problems

The day I found out I was pregnant, I broke down in tears for more than an hour. Fortunately, I was not alone. Having dialled the number I saw on the sign, a week later I sat in the small room of a Christian Charity Centre in Springfield, New Jersey. I saw two red lines instantly appear on a little white stick. Can you believe, even after the first pregnancy test came back positive, between tears I instructed the sweet older lady to perform a second test, as I did not want to believe what I could see clearly with my eyes. Check please! I had officially switched off and turned my denial dial right up. The lady reassured me the test was accurate, and I could expect to give birth on October 31st, 2012. HOTT DAMN! That was my birthday! This was beyond freaking me out, and I had no idea if I could even go through with the pregnancy. What was a girl to do? Perhaps take a deep breath and trust everything was as it should be. And it was; I simply could not see beyond my own fear.

***

I decided to name my baby Jevon out of desperation, if I am being completely honest. We were registering him the next day and I was far from impressed with his father's idea to have him be a Jr. And he was not keen on the names Kyron, Aiden, Josiah, or even Jordan. Before you call me wrong, we compromised. I was so shocked to find out six years later the name Jevon means 'gift of God'. He really is my miracle baby. I beat myself up for years about getting pregnant, until my mentor Joanna helped to shift my perspective from one of pain and judgement to one of gratitude for the little person that called me mummy. Seems like this disappointment was a divine appointment.

First and foremost, I am grateful, as pregnancy revealed I was born with a rare genetic condition where only one half of my uterus was formed. I have only one fully-formed fallopian tube and the other, which never developed, was removed after the baby was born. This condition went undetected for twenty-three years, but little Jevon alerted the doctors to what was going on within, helping them to prevent a future ectopic pregnancy, cancer, as well as provide specialised care for the last four months of my pregnancy and bring a healthy baby boy into the world.

Second, I had the guilt of becoming a mum for years because I felt I was on the path to a successful career, only to have my world come crashing down right before my eyes. After much personal development, space to reflect, journaling and inner work, I came to the realisation that before giving birth, I was slowly beginning to lose myself and had neglected my relationship with God. I was not doing my inner work and I was not developing myself mentally, spiritually or even emotionally. Rebuilding my life with a child now a part of it enabled me to refocus on living a life with purpose, reconnecting with God, learning to love myself unconditionally and doing work that impacts the world and lights me up in the process. I also believe the experience of feeling stuck and losing who I was – *now that I am on the other side* – enables me to powerfully support other women going through similar experiences.

Children are blessings, yes! But it does not change the fact that some days I feel like giving my son full permission to act as the adult he attempts to be and simply crawl back to bed to watch Netflix and chill. There are also times when Jevon's mood swings, unpredictable behaviour and outbursts have me wanting to scream (which I often do). Regardless, his innocent laugh, beautiful smile and caring nature allow me to witness what it means to be blessed, and I am forever thankful for my gift from God.

# LET US EXPLORE

We are often so busy chasing our dreams, worrying or simply surviving that we allow the most important moments to pass us by. Take time today to sit and journal on the questions below

Do you feel fully present as a parent?

_____

_____

_____

_____

_____

Are there any beliefs/stories you need to let go of to be more present as a parent?

_____

_____

_____

_____

_____

Can you, will you and when will you let go of the above?

_____

_____

_____

_____

_____

**Write down five ways you can enjoy more time spent with the children**

1. _____
_____

2. _____
_____

3. _____
_____

4. _____
_____

5. _____
_____


**Write down five ways your children have been a blessing in your life**
*(When motherhood feels challenging, look to what you have written below and remember how blessed you are)*

1. _____
_____

2. _____
_____

3. _____
_____

4. _____
_____

5. _____
_____

# PART FIVE

# Life Lessons
# on Being a Perfectly Imperfect
# Woman

A perfectly imperfect woman: who is she? What does that mean? 'I have spent my whole life focusing on perfection and now Nofisa, you call me imperfect?' I hear you, I really do, and here is my answer.

From the outside, many will look at my life and call me Wonder Woman, and I am over here like no, it is not easy at all. I often do not feel like I have it together. I am currently juggling a full-time job, raising my six-year-old son without a father that is physically present, writing, coaching, teaching pole, dating sporadically, making time to exercise and keeping up with my hobbies, which can often feel overwhelming. Most days I fall asleep putting Jevon to bed and wake with a pile of unfinished business. Regardless, every day I wake focused on being the best me. Well, most days; some days I just want to go back to sleep and hide from my priorities and responsibilities. This is all part of the journey called life. I have relinquished any attempts at letting people think I am a well-oiled machine that does not have bad days, because that is not real. First and foremost I am human. Second I am a woman; an emotional creature, so there are days when I am going to get into my feelings too. However, I have written this book as a way of embracing all of me; the good, the great, the flawed, the passionate, the individual who makes mistakes, the perfectly imperfect woman.

A perfectly imperfect woman is also you, my dear. She is your mother, aunts, sisters, and daughters, your cousin and your best friend. A perfectly imperfect woman has unhealed wounds, yet she is learning how to be the best she can from where she is. She is learning to love herself as she walks the journey called life and, at some point, will (if not yet) realise she is enough and worthy of all her heart desires. From one woman to another, a big realisation for me was that we are exactly where we need to be in this moment, and what we do from here, the choices we make today, will determine how we live moving forward.

*\*\**

My journey from childhood to womanhood has been nothing short of interesting, awkward, scary, challenging, fun, eye-opening and magical. The most challenging was not owning my own beauty or knowing how to love all of who I was. I spent the best part of my teenage years hiding and unwilling to look at the reflection staring back at me. On one hand I was confident, outgoing and a social butterfly but, like day and night, I also avoided looking people in their eyes as well as in the mirror at all costs. I would also stay inside for days when my skin erupted, leaving my face scattered with blemishes; whiteheads, blackheads and the most painful boils. I suffered from severe acne for approximately eleven years and still suffer from scalp psoriasis today. To some it may be nothing; it certainly felt that way to my mother, who reminded me regularly 'people are starving and dying in Africa and you are complaining about your hair and skin'. I can understand what my mum was attempting to do, yet these types of comments did little to help me escape the self-loathing I found myself in at the height of being a teenager.

Constantly being compared to the sun and Lisa Simpson because of my complexion also played a part in the struggle for self-acceptance. Also, I felt uncomfortable around the man who was supposed to love me unconditionally, to the point I would not want to be in my father's presence as it felt like he always made a point to highlight my flaws.

'Nofisa, you have a large spot on your nose.' *Oh I only just spent the last three hours trying to cover it up and debating whether I should leave my house or not, but thank you for letting me know.* Then there were the times I would have my hair back and he would ask what happened to my hair as I looked like I did not have any. These are comments my father would probably dismiss today, but they made me feel ugly and doubt my true beauty as a young adult.

The personal development work I have undertaken, over the last three years especially, has helped me to know and love who I am on a much deeper level and has lessened the crumbling effect other people's words had on me. In fact, if I really think about it, as I have changed the way I feel about and view myself, the world shifted and my experience with people is a much more loving one. Yet I know this is only possible because of the changes I made within myself first.

The self-love and acceptance journey can be challenging, yet I wholeheartedly believe the destination is worth it. Some individuals are still asleep to their greatness, power and potential within, but it does not change who they are at the core, perfectly imperfect and worthy of all their heart's desires. The rest, they are wide awake to the blessings life hands out freely and have begun to shake many others from their lifelong nightmare. My only hope is that if you are still asleep to life's magic, your wake-up call comes sooner rather than later. The world needs both you and I to become who we were called to be, to carry out the work only you were called to do in your own perfectly imperfect way.

# CHAPTER 27

# Life Lesson Twenty-Seven

## FUCK IT, I AM 30

This chapter is dedicated to an attitude I am wholeheartedly adopting as I sashay into my next decade. I have (and you may have too) spent too many years worrying, living in fear and stressing over what other people think about the way I desire to live my life. I am over it. 'Do You Boo' is the new motto, and I invite you to join me.

### Do Not Let the Opinion of Others Keep You From Your Passion

I am a pole dance instructor and I love it. The 'Power of Pole' is real. Supporting an individual to move from fear to being in her power and confidently working the pole is a pleasure to watch, as empowering others is what I do, and doing this through pole dance is no exception.

Yet, can you believe it took six years from initial desire to pole dance, to taking my first class. Why? I allowed the comments of my then boyfriend and the fear of being judged to shatter my confidence and keep me from taking the first step. I remember telling him with excitement I wanted to pole dance, and he let me know with an irritated look I would be a 'whore' if I chose to explore that activity. No sixteen-year-old wants to be called out of her name in that way, so I shoved that desire deep down into the pit of my body and kept it moving.

With hindsight, I should have let him go instead of the dream but, hey, we live and we learn. At the age of twenty-two, while still living in New Jersey, I decided to try a pole class. This desire was not going anywhere. I refused to put it off for another moment and, OMG, was I hooked from day one. It was about time I unleashed a side of me that had been hidden and neglected for so many years.

Regardless of my happiness, I would often get disapproving comments about taking on pole dance. My mother became uncomfortable as my interest in the sport heightened and I was spending more time at the studio. She was concerned I was being 'too sexy' and no longer looking at it as a sport. *What a way to stamp out a woman's femininity*, I thought. I felt as though my niece's mother looked down on me after learning of the new-found passion, from the tone of her voice when she once asked, 'Are you really going to do that?'. Errr, yes, yes and YES. I am pretty sure my brother felt embarrassed at the time to share with others what I was up to when people back home in London asked about me, yet I did not care. I was fulfilled and refused to let others talk me out of the very thing that brought joy to my life.

Worrying what people thought about me and my life choices also kept me from really going for it in my coaching business in the early days. Would they think I was annoying by reaching out to share my new business venture? Would others avoid me now because they thought all I would do is talk business or how I could help them? I allowed the fear to become bigger than my why, and procrastinated on letting the world know what I was up to.

Today, pole dance remains my escape; it is a safe place to develop confidence and self-esteem. I was not trading that in just to avoid judgement and other people's criticism, and neither should you if you have found something you love to do.

I have learned what matters most is that you are happy doing what sets your soul on fire. You are always going to come across negative Nancies, whatever you decide to do. You cannot allow what others think to keep you from what you love. Decide, commit to the process and trust that you will be supported along whichever journey you choose. It simply may not be the support you were looking, hoping for or expecting. Accept it and know that the universe has your back; these desires were put within you for a reason; go ahead and 'Do You Boo'...

**The world is waiting for all you have to offer**

# LET US EXPLORE

What is the No.1 activity you have been putting off for fear of what people will think of you?

_____

_____

What fears/beliefs do you need to let go of to take the next step?

_____

_____

What date will you take your first step?

_____

_____

What emotions/thoughts are coming up as you get ready to take a leap?

_____

_____

_____

What support would you like to receive along the way? (_Remember, when the student is ready the teacher appears_)

_____

_____

_____

# CHAPTER 28

# Life Lesson Twenty-Eight

## LIFE IS NOW

*'When I move back to the USA is when life will begin.'* This, I am embarrassed to admit, was my dominant thought process throughout the latter part of my twenties. I truly believed life could not be exciting while living in London. Desperate to make the move yet never taking real life action to manifest this desire, I was holding on to future dreams and neglecting all that I had and was capable of in the present moment. I have since learned and appreciate that life really is now. I am not saying YOLO (you only live once), go live recklessly and abandon all sense of responsibility. Nope, I simply mean it is important to be present and revel in the magical moments of life. We tend to miss these moments as we hold off our happiness for a time in the future when we hope conditions will be different.

Are you guilty of putting off pleasurable activities or living life exactly how you desire until;

- *You lose weight*
- *You find the one*
- *You move to another city*
- *You make more money*
- *Your business takes off*

- *You get married*
- *You make new friends*
- *Your schedule is less hectic*
- *You get a new job*
- *You are more confident*

You can fill in the blanks. The point is, there are so many of us missing out on living our best years because we hold on to this toxic thought process. I have a friend who recently relocated for a cool opportunity in the music industry. We briefly caught up on the phone last week and I asked him how it was going and if he loved what he was doing. His response was 'meh', followed by him pointing out that without a special lady he could simply not enjoy living his best life. My response? 'Switch that mindset around'. Remember, feeling good and enjoying exactly where you are right now will attract the relationship you desire, not the other way around.

## Are You Pleasure Starved?

Want to know what happens to women who grow up and forget to have fun in their daily lives? Oh yes, they develop what I call 'all dried up syndrome'. It can have devastating effects in your life, such as causing you to feel bored, alone, fearful, unfulfilled, to hold on to resentment, lose your glow and focus on what you do not want. #scaryshit.

What I love about adding more fun to the day is that for each individual reading this, it will mean something completely different. Fun is defined by you. I can create pleasure by simply blasting the music in my home and doing chores, attending a dance or gymnastic class, going to the movies or reading a book. What is fun for you? Regena Thomashauer says most women are focused on the opposite of pleasure, and now is the time to redesign your life, making pleasure a priority. Entertain yourself, find pleasure and fun in the small things as much as you do in the big events of your life. Take a new class, join a club, create a group of like-minded individuals, network, read, shop (or window shop), take cooking lessons, have coffee with friends, do what you desire.

*'We can resist pleasure so effectively because most of us have this odd little interior voice that says if we work hard enough, we will get pleasure someday.'*

**~ Mama Gena ~**

Again, life is now, and we must not spend another minute forgetting we can enjoy even simple pleasures in the present moment instead of waiting for conditions to change. I believe as you move toward a more pleasurable existence, all you are seeking will accelerate toward you.

Now for those reading and fighting the need to say something like, 'I don't have time, money or even childcare to have fun right now,' I call bullshit. You do not need money to start adding pleasure to your day. You can ask a friend or family member to take care of your children for a few hours or enjoy an activity with them. You most definitely have the power to create the time to spend building plenty of fun into your days. So, the real questions are:

- *Would you like to consistently live in the moment?*
- *Are you ready to make yourself and pleasure a priority?*
- *Are you ready to unlearn most of what you were taught to believe about happiness and create your own definition?*

Releasing the thought that pleasure can only begin after achieving a level of success has freed me up. I can now be, do and have the things I truly desire, unapologetically, as and when I want. Go forth and live your best life now. This is not a rehearsal, this is the real deal.

**LIFE IS NOW!**

# LET US EXPLORE

**Spice up your week by creating your go-to pleasure-boosters**

**First, make a list of the tasks you must complete at least once a week**

1. _____
   _____

2. _____
   _____

3. _____
   _____ 12215761 _____

4. _____
   _____ 84 – 00 – 04 _____

5. _____ Ekaete Ekpenyongova _____
   _____

6. _____
   _____

7. _____
   _____

8. _____
   _____

9. _____
   _____

10. _____
    _____

**Looking at the list above, take some time to create a more pleasurable way to perform each task.** *(For example, I listen to music while washing the dishes or doing spring cleaning, and watch a movie while doing my monthly haircare routine. I also love dressing up for my day job, which makes me feel awesome each day and allows me to show up in a more confident and powerful way)*

1. _____

_____

2. _____

_____

3. _____

_____

4. _____

_____

5. _____

_____

6. _____

_____

7. _____

_____

8. _____

_____

9. _____

_____

10. _____

_____

**Make sure you can commit to the pleasure-boosters by creating space in your calendar, pronto** *(You may need to wake up a little earlier if you are putting more effort into getting ready, or book yourself a fortnightly manicure straight after work. Just ensure it all goes on the calendar.)*

**At the end of the week, record how you felt about making those simple shifts on your list**

_____

_____

_____

_____

_____

_____

_____

_____

**How can you create more of this feeling in your day-to-day life?**

_____

_____

_____

_____

_____

_____

_____

# CHAPTER 29

# Life Lesson Twenty-Nine

## SPEAK YOUR TRUTH

*'Our biggest fear is not in expressing the truth but that we will be attacked or belittled because of our truth.'*

**~ Kelli Wilson ~**

There was a time when I feared speaking up and found it very uncomfortable to let people know how I really felt. Simply put, I was afraid of the consequences of speaking my truth. Would others be angry at me? Would I lose my job? Would I hurt someone's feelings? Would my partner think I was too sensitive? Would I end up alone? Those were the questions that plagued my mind and often held me back from speaking. This turned out to be to my detriment, as struggling to articulate my feelings would often lead to massive outbursts. I was the one who could do a 180 on someone in a matter of seconds, going from passive to highly aggressive, zero to one hundred, before you could ask, 'Is everything okay?' It did not feel safe to be honest with the people around me growing up, yet as I approach thirty, learning to speak my truth is a principle I wholeheartedly stand behind. So, what changed, Nofisa?

*'Learning to speak your truth sooner is one of the most important success habits you will ever develop.'*

**~ Jack Canfield ~**

227

I changed. I began to study the principles of success offered by Jack Canfield in his bestselling book *The Success Principles*, and started at once to apply the suggested methods from the chapter entitled 'Tell the Truth Faster', which was met with great success. I have learned that to tell the truth allows one to deal with things as they are and not as we wish them to be. I used to sit on my negative feelings for months, until I began to realise how often I was hurting myself by constantly replaying in my mind the conversations I was too scared to have and then beating myself up for not having the courage to speak out. That was a drag.

**I will not remain quiet just so you can remain comfortable**

## It Takes Energy to Withhold the Truth

I remember coaching a woman named Dina who could not find the courage to tell her friend she did not want to attend her Caribbean wedding, and instead wanted to visit Spain for her own personal development. Dina's way of handling the situation was to constantly remind her friend money was tight and she did not have it to spend (Dina had the money, she simply did not want to spend it on the wedding). Hence the reason she had yet to make a final decision on attending. What Dina failed to realise was that by the power of her words, she was creating situations to confirm her belief money was tight. Car repairs, lost money; there were a few incidents where Dina found herself out of pocket, and I had a strong feeling it had everything to do with her keeping the truth from her friend.

It really does take energy to keep a secret and, eventually, you are the one who suffers in some way. My treatment: It was time Dina faced her lions and told her friend the truth, that she would not be attending the wedding. To Dina's surprise, her friend totally understood and reassured her things were not going to change due to her absence at the wedding. Bingo! Dina's immediate money dramas ended and she felt good to have spoken up.

One of my most challenging areas to speak my truth was around the subject of money with my mother. It is unfortunate she has yet to do the inner work to develop a different relationship with money so, around this subject, there is a high level of fear, stress and worry. Fear of losing her home, fear of not having enough to survive, fear of going back into debt and so on. I have also grown up with limiting beliefs around money, which saw me find it very difficult to pay for some of the high-level courses I have joined in previous years.

I recall more than once being so afraid to ask my mother for financial support as she had already vowed to not give me another dime toward course fees. Feeling stuck, desperate and without the confidence to create money at will, I borrowed money without her knowledge, setting a date to pay it back before she found out. I was in the wrong, completely. It proved a challenge to keep that secret as I lived in constant worry about how she would react if she found out before I paid up. My mother did find out and she was both pissed and disappointed. A noticeable distance in our relationship was evident, yet relief was the emotion that washed over my body that day. A weight was lifted off my shoulders by everything being out in the open; the truth really does set you free.

- *Think about it, are you withholding your truth from someone who deserves to hear what is on your heart?*
- *How is that making you feel?*
- *What is the worst that can happen if they found out your truth?*
- *Do you respect that person enough to allow them to deal with things as they are?*

## Assertive Does Not Equal Bitch

When it comes to attitude, I have noticed there are often two extremes. Being a nice girl or the bitch. I have met many women who would rather be placed in the 'nice girl' category than be labelled a bitch. However, there is a third option: The empowered woman. This lady is assertive but nice, can speak her mind and still be respectful and is super-confident in who she is, so does not need outside approval to validate herself.

If you are to become an empowered woman, it is time to let go of the idea you control how people feel about you. 'I don't want to say what I am really thinking for fear of coming across as a bitch...' In every moment you are teaching others how to treat you by what you say and do, what you do not say and how you are showing up. The nice girl says nothing, the bitch says way too much and the empowered woman handles her business and says what is necessary with integrity. I kid you not, I have at one time or another been in all three categories, however the approach of an empowered woman is one of compassion, love, understanding, and a woman who knows herself, which is key to building successful and powerful lasting relationships.

Today, I feel confident to openly share my thoughts, desires and emotions with others because I understand nobody can take my power. It is I who gives it away when I become wrapped up in fearful thinking, ignore my intuition and give up on faith. When someone shares with me their struggle to tell people the truth, I always advise that when speaking your truth, if you do so with respect and integrity, you are doing no harm, for you are simply sharing what is on your heart. You are in no way responsible for the feelings, emotions or behaviour of another. This idea you are going to hurt the other person's feelings is not true. What you really fear is how you will feel in response to how they have taken the information you have shared. This is a reaction to something similar that may have happened in your past. The experience is being subconsciously remembered and causing you to react before you begin. Get it off your chest. Telling the truth enables you to become authentic, trustworthy and is a key success habit.

# LET US EXPLORE

*'Underneath all resentments are unfulfilled needs and desires. Whenever you find yourself resenting someone, ask yourself, what is it that I am wanting from that person that I am not getting? And then make the commitment to at least ask for it.'*

## ~ Jack Canfield ~

**What is the truth you have been unable to speak?**

_____

_____

_____

_____

_____

**What uncomfortable conversation do you need to have?**

_____

_____

_____

_____

_____

**Who do you need to have it with?**

_____

_____

_____

_____

_____

_____

_____

**When will you have this conversation?**

_____

_____

_____

_____

_____

**What has previously kept you from speaking up?**

_____

_____

_____

_____

_____

**What fears, stories or beliefs do you need to let go of to courageously have this conversation?**

_____

_____

_____

_____

_____

# CHAPTER 30

# The Next Chapter

So, my darlings, we have arrived at the final chapter before parting ways. Yet, for you and me, this is not the end but an opportunity to begin a new phase in our lives. One where we are bolder, unapologetic, listen to our intuition (fully trusting it will guide us on the right path), speak our truth, take more risks, grind for our dreams, live more, love more, and go after our goals like our hair is on fire.

It has been an extraordinary journey to share some of the most significant lessons which have shaped my life until now. My number one goal being to leave you better off in some way than you were before picking up this book. Also, my hope is I can inspire you to go out there and begin designing the life you truly want, just as I intend to do, day by day, one step at a time, because it is up to nobody but you to create that which you desire to experience.

## My Thirties Won't Look Like My Twenties

There are lessons attached to all our experiences. Are you looking for the lesson and the blessing or for someone to blame? Life lessons are there to ensure we grow through all that we go through and become more evolved, wise and powerful beings on the other side. We must therefore begin to take responsibility for our outcomes, to ensure we avoid repeating the patterns that keep us from living our best life.

You see, if your next chapter looks like the last, if next year looks like this year, you must question whether you are learning the lessons specific to your journey. The lessons I have shared within the pages of this book have brought me to where I am today, and let me tell you, life is getting better and better from the inside out because I have chosen to grow through the challenges of life, now looking at myself (to be the change) when things are not as I hope them to be, as opposed to making someone or something else responsible for my happiness. The more I feel good within myself, the richer my life experiences have become. I finally realise I am co-creating my reality, and if I desire more of anything, the change must begin with me and from within.

## Evolution

I can now easily recognise my limited thinking and dysfunctional patterns and find it easier to identify ways that I hold myself back from all I desire. Having an improved tool kit and skill set have also allowed me to better deal with self-sabotage, negative thinking, toxic relationships and the ability to respond with a degree of control, compassion and understanding to the events and circumstances of my life daily (there are those days when I have overreacted but, hey, I am perfectly imperfect).

I love the fact I am now more direct and open about what I will and will not accept in any relationship. Due to raising my vibration and giving myself permission to receive, in as little as months I have seen a direct impact on the quality of men I attract into my life and how they show up for and treat me. I cannot stress how good it feels to know that, through my choices, having boundaries, forgiveness work, levelling up, learning to receive, and cleaning up the relationship with me first and foremost, that I can call in an amazing man. It puts the power and responsibility in my hands, and as I have mentioned before, it is up to nobody but me to create the life I desire to experience, including the type of partner I wish to spend my life with.

It has also been extraordinary to witness a rise in my income over the last year and to experience a shift in my relationship with money. I no longer fear 'not having enough', as I have also learned that I can create money at will.

The year leading up to my 30th birthday has seen the greatest shift for me in all areas of my life and I am so full of gratitude. From the friendships I have created, the money I have made, the skills I have developed to the people I have inspired by simply living my truth and feeling more confident as a woman. Chapter twenty-nine has been awesome, but chapter thirty is going to be freaking epic.

I believe confidence is sexy and a simple commitment to living my most authentic life has seen my level of confidence rise, allowing me to do more of what makes me feel good and letting go of my fears and doubts in the process. Yet this would not be possible had I not learned how to fall in love with me first.

I have spent too many years hiding, doubting my beauty, self-loathing and wishing for my body, skin and hair to be different. Learning to appreciate and embrace all that I have and am has created a dramatic shift in the way I show up in the world. I now LOVE the woman staring back at me in the mirror, and for a long time I could not write or speak those very words. So if you see me in the street swinging my hips, strutting my stuff, feeling myself, and moving to the beat of my own happy song, know I have finally found a degree of inner peace and I refuse to dim my light for anyone. It feels so damn good to hold my head up and unapologetically stand in my truth, power, fierceness and vulnerability as a perfectly imperfect woman.

**This Is My Chapter 30…**
**What Will Your Next Chapter Look Like?**

# LET US EXPLORE

Now you have completed the book, take inventory of your life. Where are you now and where do you desire to go? Write it down and take the first step. I also ask you to ensure you are paying attention to the lessons given along your journey, as this will propel you forward. Make a commitment today to become the best version of you. I look forward to reading your story soon.

**Describe your present circumstances** *(Where are you now?)*

_____

_____

_____

_____

_____

_____

_____

_____

_____

_____

**Describe what you desire your next chapter to look like**

_____

_____

_____

_____

_____

_____

_____

_____

_____

_____

_____

**What are you willing to give up, to move toward the above?**
*(What price are you willing to pay?)*

_____

_____

_____

_____

_____

_____

_____

_____

_____

_____

_____

_____

_____

*'When you are doing what you want for the right reasons, there is a price to pay, but you will find pleasure in paying it.'*

**~ Kendall Ficklin ~**

# Epilogue

- *Will you dare to dream?*
- *Will you dare to do something different and create amazing results for yourself?*
- *Can you honestly say you are maximising your potential?*

## Embody the Principles

I have had many powerful teachers and learned a great deal, particularly over the last twelve years, but here is some food for thought before we go our separate ways. Knowledge of the success principles you have learned to date and will come to learn alone will not change your life; you must embody those principles. This is where I have fallen short in the past. Knowing is not enough; we must be, we must do, we must live it. I started in business telling others about the success habits that would change their lives because I had read about them, yet to a certain degree I had yet to allow the same principles to become a natural part of my lifestyle, so I continued to struggle and find it difficult to meet with consistent success.

Peta Kelly shares in her book, *Earth Is Hiring*, that this is where most fail to manifest all they desire. It is the challenge to embody the laws and principles that have worked for so many before them. Alignment is key to our success. I want to leave you with this... Right now you have everything you need to get everything you want. The question is *will you do what you need to do to have all that you say you desire?*

> *'It's time to start living the life you've imagined.'*
>
> **~ Henry James ~**

239

# About the Author

Mother of one, Female Empowerment Coach, Speaker and Pole Dance Instructor, this dynamic female is on a mission to support women worldwide to get unstuck, learn to love themselves and gain clarity on their deepest desires.

A woman of enthusiasm, passion and integrity, Nofisa Caseman is a certified Theta Healing® DNA Basic Practitioner, Transformational and Self-Confidence Coach. With a 'No BS' approach, Nofisa empowers her clients to get out of their own way in order to become their best self and live life on their terms... Unapologetically!

Having found pleasure in the *Art of Pole Dance*, Nofisa now holds monthly beginner Masterclasses in London, where she helps women to develop confidence, self-esteem, awaken their sensuality and walk confidently in heels.

To find out more about Nofisa's coaching program, pole dance masterclasses or to inquire about her availability as a speaker, you can contact Nofisa via:

**Email**: *info@msnofisacaseman.com*
**Instagram**: *@nofisa.caseman*

# Notes